Cromosys Publication

THE PARLIAMENT HORROR

NIRANJAN JHA SHOWMAN

Founder - Niranjan Jha Showman

Education and Technology Research Center

Patankar Park, Nallasopara (W), Mumbai. +91-9561450045

Education, Technology, Publication, Healthcare, Newsmedia, Realtor, Filmmaking

www.facebook.com/cromosys

+91-9561450045
Learn Advanced Skills
And Get Job Instantly
GERMAN
Python
FRENCH
C++
SPANISH
Java
ENGLISH
HTML5
RUSSIAN
CSS
JavaScript
Cromosys
Education and Technology Research Center
Nallasopara (W), Mumbai

Learn Web Programming
Demo-Class Free
HTML
CSS
React
JavaScript
Typescript
Bootstrap
Cromosys
20 Years of Experience
Nallasopara (W), Mumbai
+91-9561450045

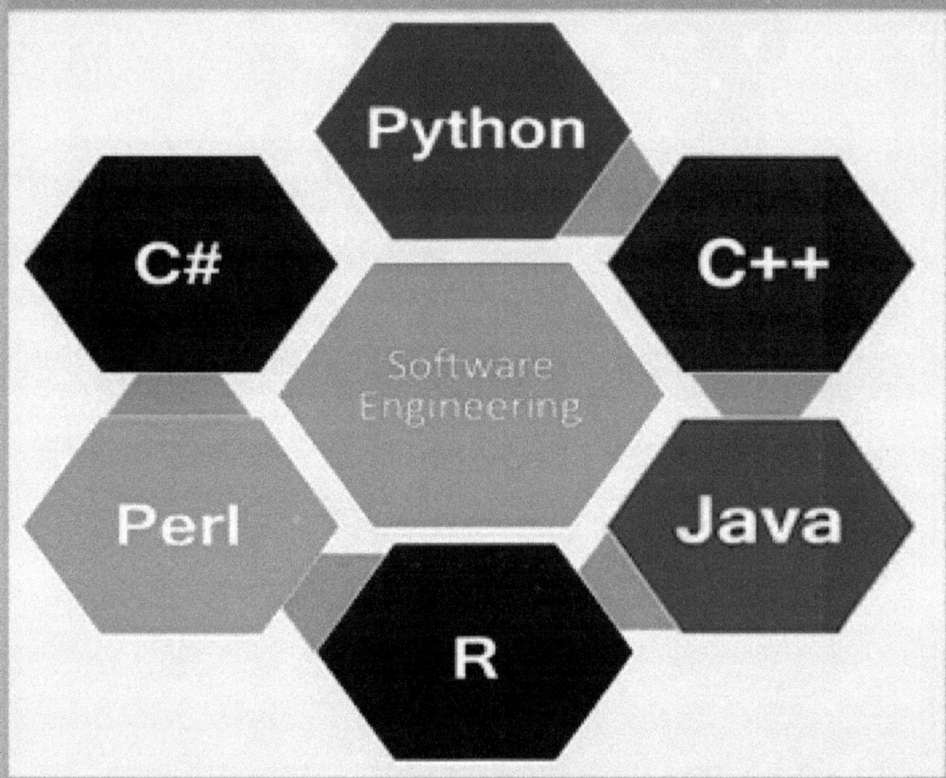

+91-9561450045
Learn Software Engineering
Demo-Class Free
Python
C#
C++
Software Engineering
Perl
Java
R
Cromosys
20 Years of Experience
Nallasopara (W), Mumbai
+91-9561450045

25 Years of Experience
Learn Visual Multimedia
Animation VFX
Movie Editing
Game Development
Cromosys
+91-9561450045
Education and Technology Research Center
Nallasopara (W), Mumbai
www.facebook.com/cromosys

Jobs Available
For Candidates Who Know

German

French

Spanish

Vacancy in Germany, France, Spain

For Hospitality, Engineering, IT Sector

With Free Visa, Airfare and Accommodation

Cromosys
Education and Technology Research Centre
Nallasopara (W), Mumbai
+91-9561450045
20 Years of Experience

+91-9561450045
Foreign Languages Institute
German, French, Spanish
Basic and Advanced - All Levels
3 x 6 = 18 Courses
FRANCHISE
Business Offer
Teaching Materials Provided
We have 1 Million Students Globally
Great Income Assured
Global Exposure
Cromosys
20 Years of Experience
Nallasopara (W), Mumbai
+91-9561450045

Cromosys Publication's

The Parliament Horror

Niranjan Jha Showman

"Hurting with truth is better than comforting with lies."
~ niranjan showman

Preface

Gujarat massacre in India happened on 27 February 2002, and following this massacre, Gujarat assembly election was dated on 12 December 2002. Mumbai terrorist attack happened on 26 November 2008, and following this attack, the parliamentary national election happened on 16 April 2009. Patna bombing took place on 27 October 2013, and following this, the national election happened on 7 April 2014. Pulwama attack happened on 14 February 2019, and following this, the national election took place on 11 April 2019. Then… when the next attack in India for general election 2024?

Who were the mastermind behind all these attacks planned a few months before elections? And why in most of them drawing result in favor of the BJP party of India? Who financed these attackers and why these attacks happened just a few months before major elections? Weren't these attacks politically planned and weren't these attacks orchestrated by the "current" ruling party of India as false-flag operations? But why? Here is the explanation.

Centuries ago… starting from Mahommad Bin Qasim, then Mahmud Ghaznavi, Muhammad Ghori and so on, these invaders never let India live in peace. Learning from these aggressors, in current era, Kashmiri terrorists initially started fighting for forceful conversion of Hindus into Islam. And after conversion was fully achieved, now they are fighting for Separatism and Caliphatism. They spent generations in fighting only. Who supported these terrorists and kept silence on their oppression? Obviously… the Congress Party of India. When the Congress Party was in power, it gave birth to Dawood Ibrahim, Abdul Latif and Mohammad Shahabuddin. And now when the BJP party is in power, it gave birth to Pragya Thakur, Kapil Mishra and Colonel Purohit. Dawood Ibrahim orchestrated Mumbai Bombing 1993, and the "he" orchestrated Pulwama attack 2019… to maintain his own Parliament Horror.

About the Author

Niranjan Jha Showman
Trainer, Author, Physician, Entrepreneur, Filmmaker, Activist

Niranjan Jha Showman is a Language Scientist and Technical Researcher. He is the Award Winning author of more than fifty educational and fictional books at Amazon. He is one of the great-grandsons of the first President of India Dr. Rajendra Prasad. He is a Public Figure, and the globally - renowned Languages Trainer of French, Spanish, and German from past twenty years. Niranjan Jha Showman is an Entrepreneur and also works as a Filmmaker in India. Being the founder and owner of Cromosys Corporation - a company located in Mumbai, India, his company is excelling in the fields of Education, Technology, Publication, Newsmedia, Realtors, Banking, and Cinemascope from past fifteen years.

Niranjan Jha Showman's good-seller educational books and novels are appreciated worldwide. He has more than one million eBook buyers online, and more than one million learners are connected to him globally. One of his novels is critically acclaimed. He is the trainer of French, Spanish, German, English Voice and Accent, and Advanced Computer Education. He is also a political activist in India.

Niranjan Jha Showman is the man who came from rags to riches, he who knows how to turn the table, and he, whom you call the man of Midas-touch. He has observed lives from the Pandora of monkeys to the sanctuary of monks, not only down-to-earth but down-to-grave. He is a B. Com. graduate, and B. Ed. from Delhi University, and diploma holder in French, Spanish and German from America. You can watch his songs, movies, educational videos and many more things by typing "Niranjan Jha Showman" in Google.

Niranjan Jha Showman
+91-9561450045
cromosys@yahoo.com
Mumbai, India
facebook.com/cromosys

Statutory
This book with its content is the registered property of the author Niranjan Showman.
The author and his Cromosys Publication holds all necessary rights of this book.
The author does not claim this book to be true or untrue.

Chapter 1
Professional Terrorism

Terrorism is a profession in Pakistan and it is so avaricious that anybody or any organization can get the attacks done by funding these terrorists. Sometimes, these mercenary terrorists don't even know who the first funder is, and without knowing this, just for money they execute the attacks in Pakistan and India. Their greed, many a times, have been misused without letting them know. This kind of misuse happens in false-flag operations when the politicians of a country stage attacks on their own country for their political gain. The examples of false-flag operations are: The Reichstag Fire (1933), The Manchurian Incident (1929), Pearl Harbor, Operation Susannah, Operation Northwoods, World Trade Center Attack, and finally... Pulwama Attack.

Yes... Pulwama Attack 2019 in India.

In Pakistan, there's a high threat of extremism and sectarian violence throughout the country. The main terrorist threat comes from Tehrik-e Taleban Pakistan (TTP), an umbrella organization of groups primarily based in Khyber Pakhtunkhwa province of Pakistan. This country is also the prime-land of the terrorist organizations such as Al-Qaeda, Lashkar-e-Taiba (LeT), Jaish-e-Mohammed (JeM), Lashkar-e-Omar, Sipah-e-Sahaba, Jaish ul-Adl, Al Badr Mujahideen, and Harkat ul Mujahideen.

But you need to know, as already said earlier, any unknown group can have an attack done anywhere in Pakistan and India by funding one of these terror outfit. They are mercenary terrorists who just pretend to be religious soldiers. They are the anarchist assemblies who work only for money covering their real face under religious blankets. And this is the first glitch that will help you understand how Pulwama attack was orchestrated for political benefit.

Daesh, a Khorasan terrorist outfit is also active in Pakistan these days. While Tehrik-e Taleban and Daesh, both groups' activities are primarily directed against the Pakistani state, they have in the past stated an intent to launch attacks on western interests. TTP and Daesh conduct attacks throughout Pakistan. Violence could be indiscriminate, including in places visited by foreigners. Previous methods of attack have included grenades, shootings, bombings and suicide bombs. Militants can launch complex and deadly attacks anytime and anywhere.

If you ask why, then you have to look into the religious framework of Islam. Islam teaches revolt more than any other religion of the world. It makes its male and female children hardcore adherent to Islamic faith by circumcision and female-genital mutilation. It strongly professes that Islam is the only true religion and others are bogus and punishable. It suggests conversion as a virtuous work and doesn't allow Muslims to live under non-Muslim rule whether monarchial or democratic. It doesn't praise much about nationhood, patriotism, democracy and cosmopolity but advocates much about Caliphism.

Because of religious inflexibility, Muslims are among the poorest of the poor in the world with around 40% of the population languishes in abject poverty – and not willing to change. For them, change is also a sin because it will weaken Islamic belief. Considering family planning also a sin, the poor Muslims' population are growing rapidly in Asia, and therefore even today, 30% of their children don't go to contemporary schools but study only religious books in mosques. When these pseudo-educated children grow, they don't get jobs. And when no job... becoming jihadi is the only option.

Foreigners, in particular westerners, are mostly targeted in Pakistan. Densely populated and unsecured areas, such as markets, shopping malls, hotels, restaurants, airports, public transport, infrastructure projects and schools are potential focal points for attacks. Foreigners need to take extra care if they plan to attend sporting events or live music venues. Attacks have previously targeted places that could be considered by militants to be un-Islamic, including music shops, theaters, and barber shops. Pakistani government personnel and institutions, and the security forces, including police, are prime targets for attacks, especially given the ongoing Pakistan military action in the areas of Khyber Pakhtunkhwa province formerly referred to as the Federally Administered Tribal Areas (FATA), which may lead to retaliatory attacks. Places of worship including churches, religious sites, minority religious sects and shrines are often targeted. Outsiders avoid religious events or gatherings and limit movements on Friday afternoons. During holy periods and vacations, there are higher risks of targeted attacks on religious minorities.

Seeing them, abhorrence is obvious as coming for Friday prayers and planning for attacks. Areas of Khyber-Pakhtunkhwa, including Peshawar, suffer regular terrorist attacks. There are reports that extremists may look to carry out attacks in the districts of Dir and Chitral, including targeting foreign nationals. There are threats of attacks in Karachi and almost daily violence. Areas of Balochistan, including Quetta also experience frequent attacks. There's a heightened threat of terrorist attack globally against British nationals from groups or individuals motivated by the conflict in Iraq and Syria.

As per popular Indian media, the Pulwama attack on 14 February 2019, a terrorist attack on Indian security forces brought the two nations India and Pakistan to armed exercise. Military action by both India and Pakistan in response to the events in Balakot could easily have led to a wider conflict between the two nuclear-armed states. Counter to some expectations, however, the conflict did not escalate and instead was successfully managed in a short period of time. Why this happened, or more accurately, why things did not get worse is not yet clear. The fog of war and statements and misstatements by both governments leave much room for interpretation.

The Western media has all but forgotten the events of February, but there are important lessons to learn from the Balakot attack. These lessons could help prevent similar events, and help put in place additional capabilities to prevent future conflicts. Just recently in 2020, a Congress leader in India named Udit Raj said that Pulwama attack was planned by Narendra Modi. He also added that there can be another Pulwama-like attack ahead of the 2024 general elections. His controversial tweet has claimed that power-hungry Prime Minister Narendra Modi had planned the Pulwama terror attack. Similar claims have also been coming from other political parties in India that Pulwama attack was planned by the BJP government to win elections citing Arnab Goswami's leaked WhatsApp Chats. While the Indian Government remains mum, Republic Media Network has rejected allegations made by the Pakistan Government related to the attack and the consequent Balakot airstrikes.

The allegations coming from foreign countries state that Pulwama attack was a false-flag operation staged by India's Bharatiya Janata Party (BJP) government for political gains. On 14 February 2019, a convoy of vehicles carrying security personnel on the Jammu Srinagar National Highway was attacked by a vehicle-borne suicide bomber in the Pulwama district, Jammu and Kashmir. The attack led to the death of 40 Central Reserve Police Force (CRPF) personnel. In response to the attack, India had undertaken airstrikes against the terror group's camps in Pakistan's Balakot. But Pakistan cited the alleged leaked WhatsApp chats of Republic TV Editor-in-Chief Arnab Goswami which claimed he knew about the airstrikes, three days in prior to the Balakot strike.

Goswami had told Broadcast Audience Research Council's former Chief Executive Officer Partho Dasgupta that it would be "bigger than a normal strike". But there has been a visible proliferation of disinformation on social media after the Balakot airstrike, attempting to show that 292 Pakistani terrorists were killed in the Indian Air Force operation. The false images have circulated relentlessly, despite the defense minister herself saying that there are "no numbers" to give out. That means Balakot airstrike claimed by India of killing 292 Pakistani terrorists is absolutely fake!

And if Balakot airstrike is fake….
Then Pulwama attack was…
A false-flag operation of the BJP party…
Instructed by Narendra Modi.

Alt News found that previously debunked images have resurfaced on social media, especially on WhatsApp, to show devastation across the Indo-Pak border in Balakot airstrike. The claims are being espoused with the help of a manufactured WhatsApp chat, which was taken down (archive) by its creator after Alt News's fact-check report.

The 2019 Balakot airstrike was popularized as a bombing raid conducted by Indian warplanes on February 26, 2019, in Balakot, Pakistan against an alleged terrorist training camp. Would you like to know the truth about it? The open source satellites imagery has revealed that "no targets" of consequence were hit. Prime Minister Narendra Modi created a stir after claiming in a TV interview that he pushed for the Balakot airstrike, despite cloud cover, as he felt the adverse weather would prevent Pakistani radar from picking up Indian aircraft movement.

There was a controversy about this statement made by Narendra Modi, ostensibly making a connection between cloud cover and the efficiency of radar. He was criticized for his statements which, according to many, lacked scientific validity. Scientists, the world over, tend to be critical of government policies and Modi is no exception. Modi, in an interview said: "The weather was not good on the day of airstrike. There was a thought that crept in the minds of the experts that the day of strike should be changed. However, I suggested that the clouds could actually help our planes escape the radars."

In simplest terms, a radar comprises of a transmitter which sends radio waves along specific directions. The signals are reflected off the target which are used to construct an image of the target. If the target is moving at a specific velocity, there is a shift in the frequency of the signal which can be used to identify the target speed. Radars detect enemy or invading aircraft even on cloudy days as electromagnetic waves from radars travel in straight line and even penetrate clouds.

The following day, Pakistan shot down an Indian warplane and took its pilot prisoner. Indian anti-aircraft fire downed an Indian helicopter killing six or seven airmen on board, their deaths receiving perfunctory coverage by Indian media. India claimed that a Pakistani F-16 fighter jet was downed, but that claim has been shown to be false. The airstrike was used by India's ruling party BJP to bolster its patriotic appeal in the general elections of April 2019. As claimed by India, the airstrike was conducted by India in the early morning hours of 26 February when Indian warplanes crossed the de facto border in the disputed region of Kashmir and dropped bombs in the vicinity of the town of Balakot in Khyber Pakhtunkhwa province in Pakistan. Pakistan's military, the first to announce the airstrike in the morning of 26 February, described the Indian planes as dropping their payload in an uninhabited wooded hilltop area near Balakot.

India, confirming the airstrike later the same day, characterized it to be a preemptive strike directed against a terrorist training camp, and causing the deaths of a "large number" of terrorists. Analysis of open-source satellite imagery by the Atlantic Council's Digital Forensics Laboratory, San Francisco-based Planet Labs, European Space Imaging, and the Australian Strategic Policy Institute, has concluded that India did not hit any targets of significance on the Jaba hilltop site in the vicinity of Balakot. Indian Prime Minister Narendra Modi has received heavy criticism while being at the helm for the last eight years. His leadership has aggravated people and made his own image negative.

Modi has superiority complex disorder because of which he thinks that he is the monarch of India. His monarchial prejudices, paradoxical speeches, ruthless decisions and power-monger conducts have created distrust among large number of Indian people. He will be seeking a third term in office in the year 2024. His party, the BJP has been putting efforts to launch a country-wide campaign to showcase its accomplishments but the opposition Congress party has been working on a campaign claiming that the government has failed to deliver its promises to the masses. Both the parties are in a race to claim power and rule in the next elections.

The terror attacks on the Indian paramilitary forces at Pulwama in Kashmir in the month of February 2019 has raised many questions on the image of Narendra Modi. Nationalist media say that it was staged by Modi because of the coming general election. As he wanted to win the next election at any cost, so he planned this attack to emotionalize people with hyper-nationalism and to make them stand against Pakistan and vote for him. The Prime Minister wanted to shove India into war until the election is over. It is true that he ruined the economy of India in last five years. A great majority of people have lost their jobs because of demonetization and tax policy of the government. People facing severe financial problem are very angry with Modi. He did nothing good to the country rather created problems. A large number of Indians have got recoiled, shocked and mentally disturbed by the oppressive leadership of him. So, Modi wanted to divert the attention of Indian people by staging this terrorist attack.

The next general election in India is in 2024. The financial condition of the county throughout the last five years remained at worst. Many businesses shut down, many people lost their jobs, and it caused many family-suicides at some places too. Moreover, some government employees are also not getting salary from past two years. The government officials say they have no money. In this condition, after two years when election comes, will Indians vote for Narendra Modi again? I don't think so, and I will not vote for him. I recollect some more reasons why I should not vote for him.

Yes some more reasons…
Not to vote for Modi…
And not to vote for BJP party…

This is the same Modi who is alleged of being the mastermind in the killing of some Hindu religious devotees in a train at Godhra, and then, started the massacre in Gujrat. It is alleged that this is the same Modi who brought terrorists to India and staged Mumbai Terror Attack. And this is the same Modi who is now found guilty of Pulwama terror attack in Kashmir. He continued shooting for a film in a park of Uttarakhand for his propaganda and publicity despite the Pulwama attack taking place in the afternoon that day. The impact of this attack was already estimated. Critics of him say that he will go to war if it means increasing his chances of winning the election. And his staunch supporters agree that India must react strongly.

Chapter 2
India Pakistan Conflict

The root of India-Pakistan conflict is essentially a Hindu-Muslim conflict. Electoral politics is more about perception and ideology of the candidates and the party, and Modi, who is greater than the BJP and its all candidates, has already won the political battle many years ago. Pulwama attack is undoubtedly an intelligence failure, Modi's foreign policy is not stupendous but the attack has helped him reap political dividends. If he goes for a war, it will help him sweep the polls. Pulwama attack, though unfortunate, has come as a blessing to him when issues like Rafale, unemployment, upper caste hegemony, and farmer's distress had cornered him.

The conflicting nature of religiosity between India and Pakistan helps Modi more than any other political leaders in India. His image of a Hindu hardliner clubbed with the hyper-nationalism and abhorrence with Muslims cultivated in majority made the public believe that it is only Modi and not any regional satraps who can take on Pakistan. Politicizing the surgical strikes in every rally and the narrative of national vs anti-national is another tactical masterpiece. In a biased perception of contemporary India, Congress is a party that indulges in minority appeasement, and the BJP is a party for the Hindus. It's a different matter that these perceptions never translated into real socio-economic gains for the communities but helped them to assert their demands. The pogrom-politics of Modi, with the legacy of Gujarat Riots, makes Hindus keep their faith in fanaticism, and so, according to nationalist opinions, Narendra Modi is not a terror-avenger but he himself is a terrorist.

In the neighboring countries of India, Modi is not seen in a good light because his name is linked with the massacres. He is alleged to have his friend-turned-foe Haren Pandya murdered who was the Home Minister of Gujarat, and his right-hand Amit Shah is found guilty in some murder cases. Earlier, he was thought about as a sincere man with a vision. He had the ability to take India to a new height. But in his five years of tenure, there has been a great collapse in economy. Those, who have gone jobless, are so much tensed that they want to fight in the name of their caste and religions. The rate of crime has increased. They have forgot the lessons of peace and nationalism. And, Modi knows this situation, so he misguides people for instability.

In 2014, Modi was successfully branded as a non-corrupt and effective administrator and facilitator of businesses with a deep commercial culture. A straightforward politician who looked after the interests of Indians. Supporters and critics alike acknowledged that Modi was a great leader. He had successfully cultivated the image of a clean politician who had reduced corruption in public life in Gujarat. While he remained repugnant to large numbers of people, particularly Muslims, human rights activists and educated urbanites, many in the Hindu majority viewed his actions favorably.

According to a survey conducted by Gallup, there has been a big decline in the percentage of Indians who rate their lives as Positively Thriving ever since Prime Minister Modi filled in the office. Both the unemployment rate, living wage, and per capita GDP has increased whereas the monthly wages for low-skilled workers has decreased. Young people are entering the workforce at a much faster rate as compared to job growth. These all facts tend to indicate an ambiguous view of the government. There were various campaigns and programs launched by the Modi Government. Clean India Campaign focused on resolving the issues of unhygienic conditions prevailing in the country. A step was taken by the government to build public toilets and promote the project through notable celebrities. Make In India is an initiative that focused on the need to bring in more innovations to increase the investment within the country itself. Jan Dhan Yojna is a scheme for people to have access to all financial services which includes credit, insurance, savings account, and pension. Stand Up India was launched in 2016 by the PM to promote entrepreneurship in India. But despite these various campaigns and programs, public life in the country is deteriorating. Confidence building measures taken by the government could not uplift the lifestyle of people. The dogmatic leaders of the BJP, given a silence-hint by Modi, could focus only on saving cows and keeping Muslims alarmed. As a result, in last five years, India fell into deep strain of unemployment, inflation and religious unrest.

Modi Government imposed high tax on people. The government thought they would pump out more money. But they forgot that less business transactions will lead to generating less income tax. This made the government system fall in lurch and lose its credit. Modi, seeing the crisis caused by himself, got involved into scams and started accumulating more money for the next election. He made many banks sick by having the loans given to his crony fugitives namely Lalit Modi, Nirav Modi, Mehul Choksi and Vijay Mallya. After getting into this slur, when he goes to deliver speeches in public, people call him a thief on his face and go out of his rally.

When the global recession started in 2008, India was being ruled over by the Congress Party, and Modi with his BJP was in the opposition. The then prime minister Manmohan Singh could poorly keep the economy in place, so by the year 2013, people started facing a lot of problems. The next year was the election year, and Narendra Modi, emerging as the leader of Hindu fundamentalism, could succeed in convincing people to vote for him. On the basis of several promises, Modi won the election but he never fulfilled any of them. For some middle class Hindus, Modi, by his attire and behavior looks like them, so they still praise him.

The hook point of his election campaign of 2014 was bringing black money from Swiss banks. Later it was discovered that the black-money holders were the real contributors to his party. Under the pretext of wiping out black money, he wiped out bank balance of ordinary people while no move was initiated against those who stashed money in Swiss banks. When people knew about it, they got flabbergasted. They felt themselves cheated by Narendra Modi. He never brought black money to India rather he demonetized Indian currencies to draw out money from the pockets of people. It created a havoc in the Indian economy and since then India is continuously slumping down into poverty.

Some people have supported the policy of the PM of high diesel and petrol prices with argument that revenue generated form high taxes is needed for the up-gradation of services and welfare schemes. They are the same Hindu despots who want Modi to retain the power in the next election. Bringing inflation down was in the agenda of the BJP, but they worked on the opposite giving hikes to the prices of everything. Though people understand that price rising up to a certain level is natural if earing also increases, otherwise it is lethal.

This is a matter of argument whether the high petrol and diesel price is a spin given to citizens to hide deep incompetence of the government and to deploy them for any tangible development project. Even after price of crude became less than half, the price of petrol has remained the same which ensured price of commodities did not fall. Modi is focusing on only saving temples and cows knowing that these heighten sensitivity of Hinduism. By the next election, he might stage the killing of his own supporter and blame Muslims. It may start a Hindu – Muslim riot favoring his electoral gain, or he will see his own downfall.

Chapter 3
Modi Supports Crony Capitalists

The government that came to power by winning a great majority in the year 2014, is now losing its ground for the next election. Don't you think something certainly went wrong? Leaving no market for business, no job for people, and no control on inflation, Modi destroyed India. He represents the crony capitalists and not the common people. What he has done since he has become the PM is that he reduced taxes of rich while increasing the taxes of common people. He is desperate about making money for businessmen such as Adanis and Ambanis by rewarding them with huge government projects in areas where they have no competence or expertise.

Few companies which have made public sector banks sick due to huge loans, his government has done nothing to make them pay their loans. These companies have legacy with Modi Empire. These same companies are also the ones with black money stashed in Swiss Banks. He even took away LPG gas from ordinary middle class in the name of giving LPG to poor people. Who stopped them from giving subsidized LPG to poor without removing subsidized LPG to middle class? This policy of him made the middle-class people of India terribly upset.

Gautam Adani has been supporting Narendra Modi for a long time. They have over a decade old friendship because their views and opinions coincide. It has been said that Adani funded the Gujrat riots, as many claim these riots were preplanned and well executed. Further, Adani supported him a lot during 2014 general election campaigns and even provided his chartered planes. Now, it's the time for Modi to favor him back and without any doubt, he has been giving his best for the last one year, meaning to say, since in his regime.

Modi travelled across the globe and bagged a lot of deals for him, for instance, he bagged $22 billion deal for him during his China visit, and auctioned coal mines for him, gets a colossal deal during PM's Australia visit as well as gets land at the cheapest rate in Gujarat. The net worth of Adani multiplies four times in just one year of Modi Government. Perceptions are quite distinct from facts. But then perceptions matter more in politics than facts. And that is why if you listen to our opposition leaders in general and the Congress vice president Rahul Gandhi in particular, one gets an impression that ever since Modi assumed office, everything in the country has been done to promote the interests of a select group of industrialists at the cost of the country's poor. If Gandhi is to be believed, the entire demonetization scheme of the Modi government is only for the benefit of the big businessmen in the country.

The counterview of this discussion about bad loans is very interesting. The data compiled and brought out by the BJP in the Parliament, as reported in The Times of India, give a detailed explanation. It is said that loans worth Rs. 36.5 lakh crore, granted to various corporates between the year 2005 and 2013, were waived off during the two successive terms of the Congress-led UPA government. Refuting the recent allegations of waiving bad loans to a few corporates, the BJP has provided data that says that ratio of bad loans had increased by 132 percent from 2005-06 to 2013-14, accusing the Congress Government.

Let us see what answer Modi Government gave to the question on bad loans. According to BJP spokesperson Shrikant Sharma, SBI had frozen Vijay Mallya group's accounts after he failed to repay loans of over Rs. 1,450 crore in 2012. However, Mallya was given loans of Rs. 1,500 crore. Adani, Ambani and Mallya were not born in the past two-and-half years.

They were supported and given loans in the regime of the Congress too. Therefore Congress owes more explanations about how these groups flourished if they had a tainted background. Obviously, there are merits in the BJP-data but giving box and cox logic does not make the government blameless. The BJP also points out the case of Reliance's heavy and costly investments in the Krishna-Godavari basin to extract gas. Let us refresh our memory how the Manmohan Singh's oil minister Veerapa Moily had decided to increase the gas price $8-8.4 against the then current price of $4.2 per million British thermal unit just few days before the UPA government was voted out in 2014. In contrast, the Modi government has imposed fines on the Reliance worth thousands of crores. These penalties can be legally challenged by the company, but the point is that it is difficult to fathom how a company perceived to be so close to the Modi government is being imposed fines, one after another, by the latter?

The fugitive liquor baron, Vijay Mallya, who is facing charges of unpaid debts, fraud and money laundering amounting to over Rs 9,000 crores told reporters recently that he met the finance minister Arun Jaitley before he left India. This allegation dated 2nd March 2016, created a storm in the Parliament. Throughout that period, Jaitley kept silent on the matter. Later, he claimed that he had never given Mallya any appointment, and so the question of his having met him does not arise. Back in London, Mallya was unfazed by Jaitley's so-called denial because the denial had only confirmed that the two had met. In June 2015, another London-based fugitive's links with a Union minister led to the washout of the monsoon session of Parliament. The British newspaper, Sunday Times, first broke the story that Indian origin member of Parliament, Keith Vaz had asked the country's immigration department to provide travel documents to the disgraced cricket administrator, Lalit Modi, since his Indian passport had been revoked. Vaz cited a request of the Indian external affairs minister, Sushma Swaraj, in the matter.

If London is the common link in the revelations on Jaitley and Swaraj, there is an uncanny resemblance between the "wise after departure" stance taken by banks in the cases of Vijay Mallya and Nirav Modi. Replies to Parliament have confirmed that the Prime Minister's Office had been alerted about the Punjab National Bank fraud as far back as 2016. Nirav Modi and his uncle, Mehul Choksi, accused in the Rs 13,500 crore PNB scam, also figured in the list of high-profile fraud cases submitted by the governor of the RBI to the PMO that year. Yet, no action was taken against the businessmen who fled the country in early January 2018. Such was their sense of impunity that Nirav Modi posed for a group photograph with the Prime Minister, Narendra Modi, at the World Economic Forum in Davos on January 23. Six days later, the PNB sent its first complaint against Nirav Modi and Mehul Choksi to the CBI, which dutifully issued a look-out notice and registered an FIR well after the duo ensconced themselves in safe havens abroad.

Narendra Modi was the self-proclaimed guard of the public's money on his campaign run as the BJP's prime ministerial candidate. He had promised to end the loot of public money. Yet, even after Nirav Modi and his family including his wife, younger brother Neeshal Modi and his uncle Mehul Choksi left the country, he managed a photograph with the prime minister in Davos. The PMO had also not acted on a whistleblower letter with extensive details about the shenanigans of the Choksi-Modi duo, which was sent in 2016.

Interestingly, the CBI registered a case against Nirav Modi, the day after the Davos summit ended. Was this a coincidence? The BJP Government launched a high-decibel damage control exercise, with ministers claiming that Nirav Modi was not a part of the PMO delegation but just snuck into the picture. This claim does not wash, as nobody can casually access the Prime Minister and accost him, either in India or abroad. The Special Protection Group (SPG) which guards the prime minister around the clock, keeps the area immediately around him sanitized, and only those who have been security cleared and whose identity has been established are allowed anywhere near. In any case, for a staged photo-opportunity where even the chairs were laid in advance, it was impossible for Nirav Modi to just photobomb. Interestingly, his uncle Choksi attended a jewelers' event, where the prime minister referred to him as brother. Imagine the kind of familiarity between both of them!

The list of fugitives that the ministry of external affairs submitted in the Parliament includes some well-known names. Among the prominent names are Vijay Mallya, Nirav Modi, Neeshal Modi, Mehul Choksi, Jatin Mehta, Lalit Modi, Chetan Jayantilal Sandesara and Nitin Jayantilal Sandesara. The lesser-known names include Ashish Jobanputra, promoter of Mumbai-based textile export firm ABC Cotspin Pvt. Ltd. Diamond trader Ritesh Jain for illegally taking Rs. 1,500 crore out of the country, Surender Singh, Angad Singh and Harsahib Singh for cheating and criminal conspiracy, Sabhya Seth for a fraud of Rs. 390 crore against Oriental Bank of Commerce; and Sanjay Bhandari for alleged tax evasion of Rs. 150 crore.

Modi is the first Prime Minister to have replaced politics of hope with politics of fear. His public speeches are replete with ambiguities, conspiracy theories and communal canards. I think it will be disastrous for the country to have Narendra Modi as the PM. His government lurches from one self-made crisis to another. Modi himself appears diminished, a caricature of his old self. Cracking a joke directed at him would have been unthinkable earlier. But cartoons, memes and jokes on him now abound and stand-up comics are increasingly mimicking him despite the backlash and trolling by the faithful. The bully in Modi is still there. And he has not lost any of his bluster. But the effect is just not the same.

He also sounds like a cantankerous, old man. Responding to the debate on the no-confidence motion in the Parliament, he famously referred to Rahul Gandhi walking across the aisle and giving him a bear-hug as the Congress president's unseemly haste to occupy his seat. It sounded like a Freudian slip. Unable to explain the dramatic rise in bank NPAs and bank frauds, he now darkly hints that the economy was in a far worse state than he suspected when he took over. He also sounds increasingly more bitter and acrimonious. Unable to tell the country that he has made mistakes or his government has mismanaged the economy, he has taken to finding scapegoats everywhere.

No Prime Minister before Modi has invested so much in projecting himself. Every time he goes out, a forty-member crew of broadcaster is deployed to beam the event live. As if on cue, all private television channels pick it up, often without acknowledging the source of the feed or the footage. He has relied on hope and hype to build a larger-than-life image. An expensive publicity machine grinds 24x7 to promote him through events, billboards, TV time, Radio talks, print advertisements, social media, WhatsApp and his seemingly endless travel.

The economy is a shambles; the prices of essential commodities and fuel have gone through the roof, the Rupee is at an all-time low, manufacturing and exports have declined, corruption in government offices remain the same and jobs are harder to get. The Reserve Bank of India's report on demonetization has finally taken the wind out of the government's shifting justifications for what is now clear was a monumental mistake. Two years later, it is now known that it did not achieve any of its avowed objectives even as it wiped out 1.5% of the GDP and millions of jobs. Amidst growing clamor for an apology from the Prime Minister, Modi is determined not to concede the folly of demonetization, which cost 100 lives, at least 1.5m jobs and left 150 million people without pay for weeks. He claims to be a religious man. That perhaps explains why his belief in this wrong-headed policy has never wavered.

He left nothing to imagination, nobody in any doubt that he was the Arch Angel himself and held Aladdin's Lamp that had the cure for everything. He claimed to have panacea but made all sick. Modi took the responsibility of all, but did nothing for sure. Black money? Wait for 100 days. Unemployment? One crore jobs a year. Manufacturing? Make in India and FDI in defense and retail. Joblessness? Trust Skill India. Slow growth? Build 100 smart cities.

Now we do know that it did not work in Gujarat, that his Gujarat Model was sham. And this is certainly not working in a large, diverse and complex country like India. Questions are being raised on the PMO micro-managing everything and his inability to delegate. Political considerations seem to outweigh administrative imperatives. He appears to believe that video-conferences with Chief Secretaries and monitoring projects by the PMO are enough to ensure implementation; that he alone can initiate reforms in education by telling students how to prepare for examinations in his radio talk. He does not seem to have the patience or the wisdom to see the damage caused by placing mediocre teachers at the helm of educational institutions. Privatization of health services and allowing insurance companies to run away with public funds is no substitute to universal and affordable healthcare.

Coming from any other leader, the promises would have been seen as reckless. But Narendra Modi managed to make them sound credible. It may not entirely be due to his acting or oratory, his reputation as event manager or even his ability to deliver spectacles. It may not also be the case that he is so cynical that he believes he can fool people all the time. To give him the benefit of doubt, he may have actually believed that he had a vision for India, that he was indeed God's gift to the country. What the country, however, has learnt to its cost is that Narendra Modi's autocratic governance skills have limitations that he tried to put the cart before the horse. The euphoria is clearly over as the country comes to terms with the disaster.

Press is no longer free and independent from past eight years in India. Not that it was any better under Congress rule. But under Modi, things have become worse. Times are tough for journalists in India, where many reporters and editors say it is becoming increasingly difficult to do their jobs. Loyalists to the country's powerful Hindu nationalist prime minister, Narendra Modi, have bullied editors into taking down critical stories, hushed government bureaucrats and shifted from the common practice of filing defamation cases to lodging more-serious criminal complaints, which can mean jail time and take years in India's overburdened court system.

Modi, popular but thin-skinned, has effectively cut off the mainstream media, forgoing news conferences to communicate directly with his vast electorate through Twitter, where he has forty million followers. India fell three spots on the World Press Freedom Index to 136th in 2017, according to the Watchdog Group Reporters. Over the years, politicians of all stripes including many from India's thriving regional parties have arrested and threatened journalists and blocked their access to information, often falling back on India's defamation or colonial-era sedition laws in an attempt to limit free speech. Many of the top news channels and newspapers are owned by families or conglomerates with business interests such as mining and telecom that have long been reluctant to be critical of the government. International observers say the situation has worsened under Modi, with media organizations self-censoring for fear of offending the government and losing valuable advertising. Modi doesn't take that kindly to criticism, and he doesn't engage with the media. The media has no real access to him at all. Two years ago, Neha Dixit, a freelancer, penned a critical report in Outlook magazine on alleged child trafficking by affiliates of the Rashtriya Swayamsevak Sangh, the Hindu nationalist organization where Modi got his start.

After a complaint from members of Modi's political party, Dixit was charged in a criminal complaint with promoting disharmony among different religious and other groups, a charge that carries a penalty of up to five years in jail. For weeks, she and her husband were the subject of online threats. Somebody published their residential address and said they should be beaten black and blue.

Today almost seventy to eighty percent of the media agencies are showing people only the things that the BJP wants. The inner credentials are hidden by these big media circuit. Congress leader P. Chidambaram alleged that there was a pervasive, systematic and infringed control over the owners of media by the Narendra Modi government. If you talk to any journalist in Delhi, they will tell you that the stories are simply killed. The control over media today is unparalleled. Maybe the control was there during Emergency, but that was an aberration. He claimed that it would be a straight fight between the Congress and the BJP in the next round of elections as there were no major regional parties in some states including Gujarat and Rajasthan.

At every 15th August, our prime ministers shout out loud that India is a free and independent country. The years keep on increasing but the ranking in freedom index keeps on decreasing. It is a matter of shame for all of us Indians where our constitution gives all the citizens of India the right to equality, freedom of speech and also not to forget we are the world's largest democracy. But today, the rights of citizens, independent media houses or journalists are bounded or set in a boundary by the government. In last four years almost 147 news channels have been banned or closed. This kind of arrogance of Modi government is not good for India in any sense. Forcing media to not speak truth will encourage Hindu fundamentalists to initially fight Muslims, and later, they will kill even Hindus. And this way, the county's nationalist image will be destroyed, as Pakistan was destroyed by religious loyalists-turned-terrorists.

Chapter 4
What Made Modi Grow

Let us see the facts that made Modi grow. Since India got independent, the Congress Party was ruling over the country, and in first three decades, the Congress won with a great majority. But increasing population and poverty was a big challenge. People were getting mobilized to fight for their own language, their own culture and their own separate state as a country. The Congress wanted to take control over it but the hypocrite people and their leaders stood against the Congress policy. The assassinations of Indira Gandhi and Rajiv Gandhi were the result of this hypocrisy. At that time, the Congress had two opposition parties, such as the Communist Party and the Janta Party.

Law goes by evidence and not by opinion of the societies. Taking advantage of this weakness of law, many belonging to religious hardline, started creating mayhem in the country. However, one has to believe in the divine justice which will punish them for their bad conduct. At least that is the belief of Hindus rather than create terrorism and justify the same. Wrong is never an answer for wrong, and eye for an eye will leave the world blind. Narendra Modi and L. K. Advani were the birds of same feather. Advani and Modi have been terrorizing thousands of innocent people in India for a long time. These terrorists are always escaping from the clutches of law because of the thread connection between Hindu terrorists and the system supposed to deliver justice.

More than 100 innocent Muslims were arrested after burning of a train in Godhra in February 2002, which in turn followed demolition of Babri Masjid in December 1992. The man mainly responsible for the demolition was L. K. Advani and Atal Bihari Vajpayee. They, to fulfill their ambition for power, played with the religious sentiments of common Hindus. Advani and Vajpayee came to power by the demolition. Following this track, Narendra Modi exploited the train-burning in Godhra to retain his power, otherwise he was sure to loose. In the aftermath of the burning train incident, the Vishwa Hindu Parishad, known as VHP, called a strike. Despite the fact that the Supreme Court had declared such strikes to be unconstitutional and illegal, and the common tendency for such strikes to be followed by violence, no action was taken by the state to prevent the strike. According to the official figures, the riots resulted in the deaths of 790 Muslims and 254 Hindus; 2,500 people were injured non-fatally, and 223 more were reported missing. Other sources estimate that over 2000 people died. There were instances of rape, children being burned alive, and widespread looting and destruction of property.

The victory of Hindus over Muslims in this riot made Modi the Chief Minister of Gujrat for the second term. The religiously sensitive ground created by Advani and played over by Modi gave the duo enormous power to politics. Both of these worthies of BJP brought utter shame to our secular tradition and secular philosophy. As a result of this conspiracy by these two men, thousands died, lakhs uprooted from their hearths and homes and many more lost everything they had and yet both are not only unpunished but are enjoying power.

The rationalization of diesel and petrol prices has added more pain of the middle class. The BJP manifesto claimed that special courts would be set up to stop black marketing and hoarding, but nothing has been done so far in this regard. Farmers still remain distressed and are committing suicides in some parts of the country due to lack of crop insurance and farmer loans. Demonetization was introduced in 2016. It was a poorly executed scheme. Currency worth Rs. 15.28 trillion had been deposited back into the banks. It clearly indicated that hoarders had found a way to legitimize most of their black money or there was no significant black money. Goods and Services Tax, GST was introduced country-wide crackdown of the illegal economy, it ended up causing a lot of misery to the general public and slowed down economic growth. Traders in the cities and towns are upset over tax bureaucracy imposed by GST. In villages, farmers are complaining of job insecurity as they feel that the government is not paying them enough for their produce. The rise of ruling party reflects a worrying trend of Hindu nationalism in India, and Modi himself has a record of stirring up Muslim-Hindu hostility.

A court in Gujarat in 2012 confirmed that the committee set up by the Supreme Court has not found any evidence against Gujarat Chief Minister Narendra Modi or 57 others in a case based on the 2002 communal riots. The report has been prepared by a Special Investigation Team headed by retired CBI director RK Raghavan. He told NDTV that he stands by his report and is ready for it to be scrutinized by anyone. He also said that the court will finally decide whether Mr. Modi should be tried. "If we are wrong, we will bow to the judgment of the court," he said.

The team was appointed by the Supreme Court in 2009; it delivered its report to the Supreme Court in May 2010. The court then handed over the case to a court in Ahmedabad and asked it to decide if Mr. Modi should be tried. The case was filed by Zakia Jafri. Her husband, former Congress MP Ehsan Jafri, was set on fire at Gulberg Society in 2002 while he was trying to protect his neighbors from a mob. Mrs. Jafri had alleged that Mr. Modi was among 62 people who colluded to ensure that assistance did not reach those being attacked.

Chapter 5
Why Gujarat Likes Modi

Many skeptics argue that the wheel of prosperity of Gujarat was already spinning when Narendra Modi had stepped in. It is a fact that, Gujarat had achieved 35% of its prosperity before Modi became the Chief Minister of Gujarat. Besides, if we take into account the industrial development of the state, it is evident that between the periods of 1960–1990 Gujarat had already established itself as a prospering state and was well ahead of the other states in terms of industrialization. Gujarat had been leading in industrial sectors like petrochemicals, pharmaceuticals, engineering, textiles, chemicals, dairy, cement, ceramics and gems and jewelry, to name a few.

From 1994 to 2002, the post–liberalization period, Gujarat's State Domestic Product (SDP) had touched an average of 14% per annum. But just as a good ship is useless without a competent captain, a prospering state can go downhill in no time in the absence of proper leadership. Gujarat today is the hub of industrialization and the state of Gujarat happens to be the first choice amongst the potential corporates, industrialists and investors. However, it is to be noted that the industrialists and investors are hardly concerned with the position that Gujarat holds in the economic development index of the states of India. It is the personality of Narendra Modi, who with his pro – business attitude and prompt delivery of validations necessary for industrialization had created the right ambience for industrialization efforts and a just work atmosphere, that they are attracted to.

When Modi had liberalized Gujarat for private investment, entrepreneurs, industrialists and investors started flocking to Gujarat. In Modi, they had found the perfect supporter of their cause for all intents and purposes. They found Modi's beckoning irresistible, not only because it was unique but also the positive attitude that Modi had towards expanding business and his bang on deliveries. The business tycoon Anil Ambani now happens to be one of the significant members of the Modi lobby and in the Vibrant Gujarat conference had actually advocated the candidature of Modi as the future Prime Minister of India in the 2014 elections.

To have an overview of Gujarat, we have to start with Chimanbhai Patel, who was the fifth Chief Minister of the state. He was with Indian National Congress and Janata Dal. He was born in 1929 in Chikodra village of Sankheda Tehsil in Vadodara district. He was elected the first president of student union of The Maharaja Sayajirao University of Baroda in 1950.

Chimanbhai was elected to the Gujarat Legislative Assembly from Sankheda in 1967 and joined the Cabinet of Hitendra K Desai. He also became the minister in the Cabinet of Ghanshyam Oza. In 1973, he replaced Ghanshyam Oza as the Chief Minister of Gujarat, and served in that office till 9 February 1974. Chimanbhai Patel was forced out of office in the 1974 by the Nav Nirman movement on charges of corruption. After being expelled from the party, he helped in the formation of Janata Morcha government in the leadership of Babubhai J Patel. He again became the CM in March 1990 heading Janata Dal-Bharatiya Janata Party coalition government. On breaking of the coalition on 25 October 1990, he managed to retain his post with the help of 34 legislatures of Indian National Congress.

He is regarded as the visionary leader and architect of Modern Industrial Gujarat. It was he who had visualized the Narmada Dam Project in his first term as chief minister and the Narmada Dam effectively was built in his second term. He considered Narmada dam as the lifeline of his state. He is the first Chief

Minister who ushered development of ports of Gujarat, refineries and power plants by private parties as part of his industrialization master plan. During his second term, he was the first Chief Minister of India to pass a bill for ban of cow slaughter and all sale of meat on all Hindu and Jain festival days.

Now we need to talk about Chimanbhai Patel and Abdul Latif who were blessed by the Congress Party around three decades ago. It's was an allegation that had shaken Gujarat's political world. A gangster, arrested in connection with the murder of former Congress leader Raoof Valiullah, had told the CBI that the killing was instigated by the late chief minister Chimanbhai Patel. The gangster was Abdul Khuddus, an associate of Ahmedabad don Abdul Latif Shaikh. But his allegation in 1993 was kept under wraps by the CBI till the daily Gujarat Samachar exposed it.

Valiullah was gunned down at point blank range in October 1992 just three days before he was to meet the prime minister to submit a memorandum exposing the increasing venality of the Gujarat Government and the alleged corruption of Chimanbhai himself. Shortly after the murder, Valiullah's widow, Vijayaben Sheth, told the prime minister that she had no doubt that Chimanbhai was behind the killing. Her suspicions was taken more seriously. Khuddus' statement alleged that Latif decided to kill the Congress leader after Chimanbhai told him that Valiullah was pressing the Centre to crack down on him. Latif lived in Dubai under the patronage of mafia don Dawood Ibrahim.

Chimanbhai's state Gujarat had witnessed some of the worst ever communal violence apart from Maharashtra. There was a spate of bombings in Ahmedabad in January, following which Chimanbhai came under fire for his inept handling of the law and order situation; he was even summoned to Delhi and given a stern warning to put his house in order. Things were bad enough for Chimanbhai when his counterpart in Maharashtra, Sudhakarrao Naik, was forced out of office. With Naik gone, it seemed as though Chimanbhai would be the next one to go.

There were many reasons why Chimanbhai remained invulnerable on this throne in Gujarat. For one, the Congress depended on him for its survival because of the majority he enjoyed in the Congress Legislature Party (CLP). Of the 98 party MLAs in the 182-member Vidhan Sabha, 66 belong to Chimanbhai's erstwhile Janata Dal of Gujarat. Of these, Chimanbhai was guaranteed the support of over 55. Under the circumstances, if pushed to the wall, he could have taken 30 MLAs with him leaving the Congress in no position to form a government.

Who was Abdul Latif? That was the time when the terror of mafia don Abdul Latif was at its peak in Gujarat and his was the most hated name in Hindu households. Having finished off all Hindu gangs in Ahmedabad, he had also emerged as a front-man in Gujarat for Dawood Ibrahim and the Pakistan ISI. The lanes of Popatiyawad in Dariyapur, in the heart of Ahmedabad, remained noisy throughout the day. Pedestrians jostle for space and two and three wheelers weave their way in and out of the snarling traffic. It was only at night that there was some relief from the endless traffic.

It was in the silence of the night, in the '80s and '90s, that trucks would make their way into the deserted lanes surreptitiously, halting briefly outside a two-storied building opposite the house of Abdul Latif, offload cartons and glide out to make way for more. The scene replayed every night for years. Gujarat had been a dry state since its inception and bootlegging was a thriving anti-social activity. Latif began his career as a gambler-turned-bootlegger, but unlike his contemporaries in the trade, he would go on to have a thriving career in organized crime.

It would not be wrong to say that Abdul Latif laid the foundations of the BJP's climb to power on its own strenght in Gujarat. It should be seen in the light of the tactic late Haren Pandya adopted to win the by-election on a BJP ticket in 1993. Pandya, who was shot dead ten years later by a terror-underworld axis, used to tell only one thing to voters: "When you go out to vote, don't forget Latif".

Haren won by a staggering 45,000 votes, riding on an anti-Congress wave among Hindu voters, owing largely to the ruling party's clear links with the mafia don. After this winning experiment, the BJP realised that Latif was a great formula. In 1995, when the next assembly election were held and the BJP fought the elections on its own for the first time, Latif became a symbolic target which resurfaced with Miyan Musharraf in 2002 and Sohrabuddin Sheikh in 2007. No election speech of a BJP leader was complete without the mention of Latif and his connections with Dawood Ibrahim and the Congress.

The BJP got two-third majority in that election and Keshubhai became the chief minister for the first time. When the police arrested Latif in 1996, Keshubhai became the king of BJP in Gujarat. It has been the BJP's formula in Gujrat to portray a Muslim as an enemy and project the party as the protector of Hindus. All this in the BJP began with Latif and moved on to Pulwama Terror Attack in 2019.

Chapter 6
Haren Pandya's Murder

Haren Pandya was the Home Minister of Gujarat. He was murdered in 2003 in Ahmedabad, when he was sitting in his car after a morning walk in the Law Garden area in Ahmedabad. He represented the Ellis Bridge constituency of Ahmedabad City as a Bharatiya Janata Party legislator. He was a member of the RSS from his early age and was also a Municipal Councilor from the Paldi Area of Ahmedabad City. Pandya was a strong supporter of Keshubhai Patel. In 1998, after the BJP came to power in Gujarat with Keshubhai as Chief Minister, Pandya was made Home Minister of Gujarat.

From this point, the twist starts that gives rising to Narendra Modi, then death to Haren Pandya, and silence to Keshubhai and Shankar Singh Vaghela to not speak anything against Modi. The political war of Gujarat started when Haren was appointed as Minister of state for revenue after Modi took over as the Chief Minister; however, he resigned from the post in 2003. Fearing that he would be denied a ticket for the 2002 assembly elections, he withdrew from the electoral fray. Later he was appointed to BJP's national executive. Haren Pandya's wife Jagruti Pandya contested on Gujarat Parivartan Party ticket in 2012 on the premise that the Modi Government was involved in the conspiracy to murder her husband. She said that her husband's assassination was a political murder.

After the Godhra riots, it was reported that in a cabinet meeting, had opposed the bringing of the bodies of the victims of Godhra carnage to Ahmedabad because that would arouse passion. He was the only person able to arrange meetings between victim's family members and Muslim leaders for Peace talk but he was shouted down at the meeting by some ministers. In November 2007, Outlook magazine reported that Pandya had revealed to the magazine in May 2002 that on the night of 27 February 2002 Narendra Modi had held a meeting in his residence in which he instructed the attending bureaucrats and police officers to allow people to vent their frustration and not come in the way of the Hindu backlash. Pandya had disclosed this information on condition of confidentiality. On 19 August 2002, Pandya again spoke to the magazine, according to Outlook, and reiterated what he had said earlier with the additional comment that if his identity as the source of this information were to be revealed then he would be killed.

The Rise of the Bharatiya Jana Sangh and latter BJP, in Gujarat can be attributed to a well-balanced socio-political alliance constructed by the RSS on ground. RSS used the Nav Nirman Movement which was a student movement against the corruption of the Congress Government of Gujarat and the Central Government of Indira Gandhi. ABVP was in the fore-front of the movement and the public march was organized for political maneuver and election, which brought victories in 1975.

Keshubhai Patel was an RSS and BJS face in the Gujarat. He won the parliamentary election and resigned to contest assembly election in Gujarat. Keshubhai became the minister in the Janta Party Government of the state. Janta Party had one more known face as Shankersinh Vaghela. Either Keshubhai Patel or Shankersinh Vaghela was to be chosen as the chief minister.

But then, Narendra Modi supported Patel and Vaghela was left with nothing. Born to a Gujarati family in Vadnagar, Modi helped his father sell tea as a child, and later ran his own stall. He was introduced to the RSS at the age of eight, beginning a long association with the organization. He left home because of his arranged marriage which he rejected. Modi traveled around India for two years, and visited a number of religious centers. He returned to Gujarat and moved to Ahmedabad in 1969. In 1971, he became a full-time worker for the RSS. Fourteen years later, the RSS assigned him to the BJP in 1985.

Vaghela was the first choice of assembly MLAs to be the CM but then Modi backed Patel. The central leadership also picked up Keshubhai over vaghela, as they were eyeing for National Election of 1996. Vaghela, for a time kept his mouth shut as he also saw his support eroding from his side. But suddenly, in September 1995, Vaghela started his rebellion with 47 MLAs and Indian National Congress was also throwing hat behind him.

The core-BJP leadership thought that was the part of a big INC plan to dismiss BJP led governments one after another. At that time Maharashtra was ruled by Shivsena-BJP, and Rajasthan was also ruled by BJP with independently. So the central leadership bowed to the demand of Vaghela and Patel was removed from CM post, Suresh Mehta was installed and Modi was dispatched to Delhi as General Secretory of the party. The central leadership under Advani was hell-bent to give a stable BJP administration for 1996 general election. But the 1996 election was disastrous for Vaghela, he lost the election. Then, he started his rebellion again, and formed Rashtriya Janata Party and INC also threw their support for him. In the month of October, he became the CM of Gujarat by INC support. But in the next year, he was removed and Dilip Parikh from INC succeeded him.

This all turmoil ended in 1998 after the clear BJP victory in the state election and parliamentary election. Keshubhai became the CM but RSS and others were not happy with him. Narendra Modi's supporters were hooting for Modi and Jana Sangh also wanted Modi as Keshubhai and his family were implicated in various corrupt practices. There were huge corrupt practices by Keshubhai and his supporters, goods meant for relief work were sent to other countries and people were openly sold in markets. It created a very bad image of Keshubhai. The breaking point came when a BJP lost the important parliamentary By-election of Sabarkanta and Sabarmati seats.

Anti-Keshubhai rhetoric became vocal and visible. Modi, who was in Delhi, his organizational skill and management was a key for BJP leadership. Kushabhau thakere and Jana Krishnamurty, both of them had a liking for Modi. They promoted Modi and Advani and Atal also supported him. As a result, Keshubhai was stumped by the central leadership and the state Sangh unit. He led a rebellion with 28 to 36 MLAs but as his position in Delhi had gone weak. His supporters had also started leaving his side. Then the final blow came from BJP state chief Rana who towed the central leadership line and Keshubhai was forced to resign for the by-election defeat and his ailing health.

In 2001, Keshubhai Patel's health was failing and the BJP lost a few state assembly seats in by-elections. Allegations of abuse of power, corruption and poor administration were made, and Patel's standing had been damaged by his administration's handling of the earthquake in Bhuj in 2001. The BJP national leadership sought a new candidate as a Chief Minister, and Modi, who had expressed misgivings about Patel's administration, was chosen as a replacement. Although BJP leader L. K. Advani did not want to ostracize Patel and was concerned about Modi's lack of experience in the government, Modi declined an offer to be Patel's deputy chief minister, telling Advani and Atal Bihari Vajpayee that he was "going to be fully responsible for Gujarat or not at all".

On 3rd October 2001, Modi replaced Patel as the CM of Gujarat, with the responsibility of preparing the BJP for the December 2002 elections. On 7th October 2001, Modi was administered the oath of office. On 24 February 2002 he entered the Gujarat state legislature by winning a by-election to the Rajkot constituency, defeating Ashwin Mehta of the INC by 14,728 votes, which enabled him to take office.
On 7th October 2001, Modi became the chief minister, on 27th February 2002 the Gujarat violence started which continued up to four months, and in December 2002 there was state election to come. The Bharatiya Janata Party led by Narendra Modi won a 127 seats, thus achieving an absolute majority in the assembly, Modi was sworn in for a second term as chief minister. Now, from past five years, Narendra Modi is the Prime Minister of India.

Chapter 7
IPS Sanjiv Bhatt and Justice Loya

Sanjiv Bhatt is a former Indian Police Service officer of the Gujarat-cadre. He is known for his role in filing an affidavit in the Supreme Court of India against the then Chief Minister of the Government of Gujarat, Narendra Modi, concerning Modi's alleged role in the 2002 Gujarat riots. He claimed to have attended a meeting, during which Modi allegedly asked top police officials to let Hindus vent their anger against the Muslims. However, the Special Investigation Team appointed by the Supreme Court of India concluded that Bhatt did not attend any such meeting, and dismissed his allegations.

In 2015, Bhatt was removed from the police service, on the ground of "unauthorized absence". In October 2015, the Supreme Court quashed Bhatt's plea for constituting a special investigation team (SIT) for cases filed against him by Gujarat Government. The court lifted a stay on his trial in these cases and asked him to face prosecution. The court observed that, "Bhatt was in active touch with leaders of rival political parties, was being tutored by NGOs, was involved in politics and activism of creating pressure, even upon

3-judge bench of this court, amicus and many others".[3]. On 20 June 2019, he was sentenced to life imprisonment by the Sessions Court of Jamnagar District in the state of Gujarat in a 1990 custodial death case. Bhatt joined the Indian Police Service (IPS) in 1988, and was allotted the Gujarat cadre. In 1990, as the Additional Superintendent of Police, he detained 150 people in order to control a riot in Jamnagar district. Prabhudas Vaishnani, one of the detainees, died of kidney failure a few days later, after being hospitalised. His brother lodged an FIR against Bhatt and six other policemen, alleging that he had been tortured in police custody. Another man, Vijaysinh Bhatti, alleged that he had been beaten up by Bhatt.

In 1996, as the Superintendent of Police (SP) of Banaskantha district, he was accused of falsely framing a Rajasthan-based lawyer in a narcotics case. It was alleged that Bhatt maliciously filed nearly 40 petitions in the high courts of Rajasthan and Gujarat as well as before the apex court to delay action against him. The Bar association members have alleged that Bhatt got himself appointed the Gujarat government's officer in-charge for the special appeal petition pending in the SC. They pointed out that Bhatt is using the Gujarat government as a shield to save himself but is also misusing the public money to fight the crimes he committed. He was accused in another custodial torture case in 1998.

From December 1999 to September 2002, he worked as Deputy Commissioner of Intelligence in the state Intelligence Bureau (India) at Gandhinagar. He was responsible for looking after the state's internal security, border and coastal security, and security of vital installations. He was also responsible for the Chief Minister Narendra Modi's security. During this period, the Godhra train burning and the subsequent Hindu-Muslim riots led to over a thousand deaths in February–March 2002.

On 9 September 2002, Narendra Modi allegedly mocked the high Muslim birth rates during a speech at Bahucharaji. Though Modi denied making such remarks, the National Commission for Minorities (NCM) sought a report from the State Government. Modi's Principal Secretary P K Mishra told The Indian Express that the State Government had no recordings or transcripts of the speech, and therefore, could not send these to the NCM. However, the State Intelligence Bureau provided the NCM a copy of Modi's speech, which had been recorded as part of routine procedure. Subsequently, the Modi government transferred the Bureau's senior officials on 'punishment postings'. The officers transferred included Sanjiv Bhatt, R. B. Sreekumar and E. Radhakrishnan. Bhatt was posted as principal of the State Reserve Police Training College.

In 2003, Bhatt was posted as the superintendent of Sabarmati central jail. There, he became very popular among the prisoners. He introduced desserts like gajar ka halwa on the jail menu. He also posted undertrials in Godhra train burning case on a jail committee. Two months after his appointment, he was transferred for being too friendly with the prisoners and bestowing favours upon them. On 18 November 2003, nearly half of the 4000 prisoners went on a hunger strike to protest his transfer. Six convicts slashed their wrists in protest. By 2007, Bhatt's colleagues from the 1988 batch had been promoted to the rank of Inspector-general of police (IGP). However, Bhatt had stayed at the SP level for a decade without any promotion, because of the pending criminal cases and departmental inquiries against him.

After the 2002 riots, a group of social activists had formed the Concerned Citizens Tribunal to analyze the riots. Gujarat's home minister Haren Pandya allegedly told this tribunal that Modi had organised a meeting at the Chief Minister's residence on 27 February 2002, after the Godhra train burning, in which over 63 Hindu pilgrims were killed. According to Pandya, in this meeting, Modi had asked the police officials not to come in the way of "the Hindu backlash". Pandya had named several police officials who attended this meeting; Bhatt was not among these. Pandya was later assassinated by unidentified men. On 14 April 2011, 9 years after the riots, Bhatt filed an affidavit in the Supreme Court of India, making similar allegations. According to Bhatt, at this meeting on 27 February 2002, Modi asked top police officials to let Hindus "vent out their anger" against the Muslims. He said that the meeting determined to bring the bodies of the Hindu pilgrims to Ahmedabad before cremation and that he had cautioned against this, fearing religious violence.

According to him, Modi's Bharatiya Janata Party (BJP) and the Hindu nationalist Bajarang Dal were stirring tensions in the city, and the Vishwa Hindu Parishad (VHP) had proposed a bandh (an illegal general strike). Bhatt claimed that the then Director General of Police, K. Chakravarthi, and the city Police Commissioner, P. C. Pandey, had raised concerns regarding the manpower available to deal with this, and both men advised that it was not wise for the bodies to be taken to Ahmedabad. Bhatt also says that he sent some fax messages to major officials soon after the meeting ended and that these referred to the meeting itself, the decision regarding the bodies of the dead and the growing activity of the BJP and Bajrang Dal. Subsequently, riots occurred in which around 1000 people died, three-quarters of whom were Muslim. Described as a whistleblower both by some of the Indian media and some pressure groups, Bhatt has since referred to the events as "state-sponsored riots" and has alleged both that Modi told his officials to be "indifferent" towards rioters and said that Muslims needed to be "taught a lesson".

In his affidavit, Bhatt mentioned six witnesses, who could testify his presence in the alleged meeting held at Modi's residence. He claimed that he had travelled to Modi's residence in the official car of K. Chakravarthi, which was being driven by Tarachand Yadav; Bhatt's driver Constable KD Panth followed them in Bhatt's official car. Bhatt's affidavit was signed by KD Panth, whose statement supported Bhatt's presence at the alleged meeting. On 24 June 2011, Panth filed an FIR against Bhatt, alleging that Bhatt had threatened him and forced him to sign a false affidavit. Panth alleged that Bhatt took him to the residence of Arjun Modhwadia, the state president of the opposition party, Indian National Congress. He further alleged that Modhwadia asked him to obey Bhatt. Panth claimed that he was on leave in February 2002, when the riots broke out, and had already told this to the Supreme Court-appointed Special Investigation Team (SIT). Chakravarthi also denied that Bhatt was present in the meeting.

When questioned why he had not made these revelations earlier, Bhatt stated that in 2004, he "started sending out feelers" that he wanted to be cross-examined by the Nanavati Commission, but the commission had not called him. In May 2011, Bhatt repeated the allegations made in his affidavit when he was called to give evidence to the NMC. Before this appearance and to support the statements that he would make during it, Bhatt had attempted to obtain documents as evidence from the police and the State Intelligence Bureau, as well as from the SIT hearing. He again requested this information in December 2011, claiming that it was needed so that it could be placed on the official record. These requests for information failed, and Bhatt alleged that this was because the Modi government opposed them because it was involved in a "cover-up". In 2012, he alleged that the NMC had consistently refused to demand production of the documents, despite Bhatt's belief that it has the legal powers to do so.

In March 2008, the Supreme Court had appointed a Special Investigation Team (SIT), headed by former Central Bureau of Investigation chief R. K. Raghavan, to investigate cases relating to the various incidents that had occurred during the 2002 riots. One of those who died in the Gulbarg Society massacre that formed a part of the riots was Ehsan Jaffri, the former Indian National Congress Member of Parliament. His widow, Zakia Jaffri, subsequently became concerned about the involvement of senior officials in allegedly aiding and abetting the rioters and by the lack of legal action against them by the police. She petitioned the Court, alleging criminal conspiracy, a "deliberate and intentional failure" to protect life and property, and failure to fulfil their constitutional duty. In 2009, the Court responded by directing the SIT to investigate the actions of Modi and 62 other people, including Pandey and some VHP leaders. Bhatt presented evidence to this particular SIT investigation in 2009.

On 13 October 2015, a bench comprising Supreme Court Chief Justice H L Dattu and Justice Arun Mishra ruled Bhatt's allegations against the SIT as totally "false and baseless". It further rebuked Bhatt, ruling that "He had exchanged e-mails with rival political party leaders and was being tutored by the lawyer of an NGO and its activist... The petitioner has even sent e-mails to influence the judicial proceedings of a 3-Judge Bench of this court and has tried to influence the amicus curiae."

On 8 August 2011, the Gujarat government suspended Bhatt, accusing him of unauthorized absence from duty, not appearing before an inquiry committee and using his official car while not on duty. Bhatt claimed that he was unable to report for work because he was required to attend various legal and investigatory hearings, including those of Nanavati-Mehta commission (NMC) – originally known as the Nanavati-Shah Commission – which had been established by the government of Gujarat.

The allegations in Haren Pandya murder case. The Gujarat government had originally appealed the court to drop charges against Bhatt and other policemen in the 1990 custodial death case. However, after Bhatt's affidavit against Modi, the Government withdrew its application, and the court initiated criminal proceedings against the policemen. On 18 September 2011, the Gujarat Home Ministry charge sheeted Bhatt in the 1990 police atrocity case. On 27 September 2011, Bhatt appeared before the Gujarat High Court in the police atrocity case against him in Jamnagar district. During the hearing, he told the Court that Narendra Modi and his former Home Minister Amit Shah had pressurized him to destroy crucial evidence in the Haren Pandya murder case.

In a fresh affidavit, Bhatt made detailed allegations against Modi and Shah. He claimed that while posted as Superintendent of the Sabarmati Jail in 2003, he had met Asgar Ali, an accused in the Haren Pandya murder case. Ali allegedly told him that Pandya had been killed by Tulsiram Prajapati (who was later killed in a fake encounter in 2006). Bhatt claimed that he had immediately informed Home Minister Amit Shah about this revelation, but Shah asked him to destroy all documentary evidence related to this matter. He claimed that he had been removed as the Jail Superintendent because he had refused to obey Shah.

On 30 September 2011, Bhatt was arrested, following an investigation into KD Panth's FIR. Bhatt alleged that Panth was following "diktats" from the Modi government, an allegation denied by Panth. Bhatt's arrest was condemned by the Congress leaders and human rights activists, who accused the Modi government of persecuting Bhatt. The arrest gave rise to protests at places such as Ahmedabad, Delhi and Bangalore. The Gujarat IPS Officers Association also expressed their support for Bhatt and his family, although this was far from being unanimous and was downplayed by various senior officers. Bhatt has referred to being harassed by members of the Gujarat police.

On 17 October 2011, Bhatt was granted bail by a local court in Ahmedabad, on condition that he continue to cooperate with investigations into the allegations laid against him. His bail application had been opposed by the Modi government. The Supreme Court suspended the case in April 2012, with Bhatt arguing that the arrest was "politically motivated".

A former BBC journalist, Shubhranshu Choudhary, filed an affidavit in November 2011 that supported the claim that Bhatt was present at the 2002 meeting. In the same month, he requested that the SIT allow his testimony to be recorded in the presence of a magistrate as he believed that his earlier statements to it had been distorted. He made several similar requests thereafter. In January 2012, the SIT demanded the original copy of the fax messages that Bhatt claimed to have sent after the 2002 meeting and which, according to Bhatt, substantiated his presence at the meeting. Bhatt said that he had already provided the evidence in 2009 and again in 2011. He also noted that the SIT could get the information from the SIB records, and he claimed that the SIT was failing to interview police officials who could testify to his movements on the night in question. This was not the first occasion that he had alleged the SIT was reluctant to examine key witnesses who could verify his whereabouts at the time of the meeting.

On 13 October 2015, a bench comprising Chief Justice H L Dattu and Justice Arun Mishra dismissed Bhatt's plea and ordered a speedy trial to be conducted in both cases. It used email evidence to rule that Bhatt had deliberately colluded with leaders of the opposition Congress Party, NGO activists and certain elements in the media to furnish false evidence about his attendance at 27 February 2002 meeting chaired by Modi so that he could falsely allege that Modi had incited riots. Bhatt contacted Pratibha Patil, the Indian President, in April 2012. He sought a probe against Modi. He has requested the center to appoint two member commission to enquire the role and conduct of Modi, his officials and police officers in the Godhra massacre. He also demanded an investigation into the government's measures on the rehabilitation for victims.

After the official release of the Amicus curiae's report, The Times of India described Bhatt as pivot in the case against Modi. Bhatt criticized the published SIT report on the Godhra attack, claiming that the SIT was shielding Modi. Besides his deposition before NCM, Bhatt has filed an affidavit in National Commission of Minorities (NCM). In his affidavit Bhatt has asked the rights panel to initiate action against the SIT headed by R K Raghavan for incorrectly recording his statements or tweaking them to give a clean chit to Chief Minister Narendra Modi. He also alleged that certain very crucial portions of his statement, including the timings of extremely consequential meetings with the chief minister Narendra Modi on 27 February & 28 February 2002, have either been incorrectly recorded or deliberately tweaked by the SIT, possibly with the ulterior motive and intent of shielding certain powerful persons including the chief minister from legal punishment.

Concerns have been raised at various times regarding the personal safety of Bhatt. At the time of filing his Supreme Court affidavit in April 2011, Bhatt requested the Court for protection and the Gujarat government assured the Supreme Court that it would provide personal safety arrangements. This situation had arisen because Bhatt believed that the SIT had passed on his testimony to the state government and thus he feared for the security of himself and his family. His wife, Shweta, alleged that there was harassment during the period that he spent in jail under arrest in October 2011. She requested that the Ministry of Home Affairs (MHA) of the Government of India intervene to ensure that both he and his family were protected. The MHA instructed the government of Gujarat accordingly.

Bhatt had been provided with two personal guards but considered this to be insufficient. In November 2011 he requested improved security, including provision of a bullet proof car. He repeated his demands in February 2012, when he also raised objections on personal safety grounds to a request from the Gujarat police that he should return his service revolver. In November 2013 Bhatt alleged that city police was not providing him adequate security, and there was an increased threat to his and his family members' lives from the "right-wing fundamentalists and the supporters of Narendra Modi". Earlier, Bhatt had alleged that his security had been downsized. The office of Commissioner of Police Shivanand Jha said that after the assessment of threat perception, it was decided that Bhatt should be provided with two armed personal security officers. However, Bhatt wrote to the commissioner, saying that he was being "provided with only one armed PSO".

Brijgopal Harkishan Loya was an Indian judge who served in a special court which deals with matters relating to the Central Bureau of Investigation (CBI). He was presiding over the Sohrabuddin Sheikh case during which he died on 1 December 2014 in Nagpur. A bench of the Supreme Court of India, headed by the Chief Justice of India Dipak Misra, on April 19, 2018, dismissed the public interest petition (PIL), and stated Loya's death to be natural and such petitions to be an attack on the Judiciary. In June 2014, Loya was appointed to the special CBI court on the Sohrabuddin case. Loya allowed Amit Shah, the accused of ordering the murder of Sohrabuddin, who is the national leader of the Bharatiya Janata Party (BJP), to be present in the court. When Shah did not attend a hearing on 31 October, even though he was in the same city, Loya ordered Shah's lawyers to ensure that he would be present at hearings when he was in the state, and set the date of the next hearing to 15 December, when the verdict would be given.

As per the report, Loya travelled to Nagpur to attend a wedding function on 30 November 2014. He stayed at Ravi Bhavan, a state government guest house in Nagpur. On the morning of 1 December 2014, at around 4 am IST, he developed chest pain and was taken to two hospitals. He died at 6.15 am of cardiac arrest. His body was taken to Latur by a family friend. Loya's family claimed that they had seen blood stains on Loya's shirt collar. Medical experts disagreed over whether this was a result of the post-mortem examination. On 30 December 2014, Loya's successor in the special CBI court, M. B. Gosavi, dismissed all charges against Shah in the Sohrabuddin Sheikh case, and ruled that he need not stand trial.

Justice Loya died in 2014, but the issue rose to limelight after Caravan Magazine published an interview with Loya's family on 20 November 2016, in which they raised concerns over his death. Loya's sister claimed that Justice Loya was under immense pressure from the then Chief Justice of the Bombay High Court, Mohit Shah. She alleged that Justice Mohit Shah offered Justice Loya a 100 crore bribe to give a favorable verdict. The family also raised concerns over the medical reports of Justice Loya, leading to a PIL in the Supreme Court of India. During a Press Conference, the Congress claimed that two other associates, with whom Justice Loya had shared the details of the case, died under mysterious circumstances as well. One of them, was lawyer activist Shrikant Khandalkar and another retired judge Prakash Thombre.

Chapter 7
Bilkis Bano case

Bilkis Bano was brutally gangraped during the communal violence that followed the Godhra train-burning incident. She was 21 years old at the time, and five months pregnant. Seven members of her family were killed by rioters. Eleven men who were sentenced to life imprisonment in the Bilkis Bano gangrape case of 2002 were released from Godhra sub-jail on 15 August 2022 after a panel set up by the Gujarat government approved their application for remission of the sentence.

Additional Chief Secretary (Home) Raj Kumar said the remission application was considered because the convicts had completed 14 years in jail, and factors such as "age, nature of the crime, behavior in prison and so on". Bilkis was accompanied by her daughter Saleha, who was three-and-a-half years old at the time, and 15 other members of her family. They fled fearing a re-run of the arson and looting that had taken place in their village on the occasion of Bakr-Id. On March 3, 2002, the family reached Chapparwad village. According to the chargesheet, they were attacked by about 20-30 people armed with sickles, swords, and sticks. Among the attackers were the 11 accused men.

Bilkis, her mother, and three other women were raped and brutally assaulted. Of the 17-member group of Muslims from Radhikpur village, eight were found dead, six were missing. Only Bilkis, a man, and a three-year-old survived the attack. Bilkis remained unconscious for at least three hours after the attack. After she regained consciousness, she borrowed clothes from an Adivasi woman, and met a Home Guard who took her to the Limkheda police station. She registered a complaint with Head Constable Somabhai Gori who, according to the CBI, "suppressed material facts and wrote a distorted and truncated version" of her complaint.

Bilkis was taken to a public hospital for medical examination only after she reached the Godhra relief camp. Her case was taken up by the National Human Rights Commission (NHRC) and Supreme Court, which ordered an investigation by the CBI. The CBI concluded that the post mortem examination was carried out shoddily in order to protect the accused. CBI investigators exhumed the bodies of those killed in the attack, and said that none of the seven bodies had skulls. How did the trial in the case proceed? The trial was moved out of Gujarat to Maharashtra after Bilkis Bano received death threats. In the Mumbai court, charges were filed against 19 men, including six police officers and a government doctor. In January 2008, a special court convicted 11 accused of conspiring to rape a pregnant woman, murder, unlawful assembly, and of charges under other sections of the Indian Penal Code. The Head Constable was convicted of "making incorrect records" to save the accused.

Seven persons were acquitted by the court, citing lack of evidence. One person died during the course of the trial.The court held that Jaswantbhai Nai, Govindbhai Nai, and Naresh Kumar Mordhiya (deceased) had raped Bilkis, while Shailesh Bhatt had killed her daughter, Saleha, by "smashing" her on the ground. Others who were convicted are Radheshyam Shah, Bipin Chandra Joshi, Kesarbhai Vohania, Pradeep Vohania, Bakabhai Vohania, Rajubhai Soni, Nitesh Bhatt, Ramesh Chandana, and Head Constable Somabhai Gori.

In May 2017, the Bombay High Court upheld the conviction and life imprisonment of 11 people in the gangrape case, and set aside the acquittal of seven people, including the policemen and doctors. In April 2019, the Supreme Court directed the Gujarat government to give Rs 50 lakh as compensation to Bilkis within two weeks. She had refused to accept the compensation of Rs 5 lakh, and had sought exemplary compensation from the state government in a plea before the top court.

Now in 2022, on 15 August, 11 convicts who were serving life sentences for rape and murder in this case, walked out of prison to a heroes' welcome. A video that has since gone viral showed the men lined up outside the Godhra jail while relatives gave them sweets and touched their feet to show respect. Bilkis Bano, in a statement, called the decision to free the men "unjust" and said it had "shaken" her faith in justice. "When I heard that the convicts who had devastated my family and life had walked free, I was bereft of words. I am still numb," she said.

"How can justice for any woman end like this? I trusted the highest courts in our land. I trusted the system, and I was learning slowly to live with my trauma. The release of these convicts has taken from me my peace and shaken my faith in justice," she wrote, appealing to the Gujarat government to "undo this harm" and "give me back my right to live without fear and in peace".

A senior official said a government panel had approved the application for remission as the men - first convicted by a trial court in 2008 - had spent more than 14 years in jail, and after considering other factors such as their age and behavior in prison. The decision had caused massive outrage in India. It's been criticized by opposition parties, activists and several journalists, who have said it discriminates against India's minority Muslims. Attacks on the community have risen sharply since the BJP formed the federal government in 2014.

More than 6,000 activists, historians and citizens had issued a statement urging the Supreme Court to revoke the early release of the convicts, describing it as a "grave miscarriage of justice". Many also pointed out that the release is in contravention of guidelines issued by both the federal government and the Gujarat state government - both say that rape and murder convicts cannot be granted remission. Life terms in these crimes are usually served until death in India. But how come the rapists got free? Isn't it a grace bestowed from "him" who maintains Parliament Horror in India and the entire nation is seeing this as a silent viewer? And isn't "he" well taught from the history of riots in India and orchestrate his own?

Chapter 8
History of riots in India

1927 Nagpur Riots
The Nagpur riots of 1927 were part of series of riots taking place across various cities in British India during the 1920s. Nagpur was then the capital of Central Provinces and Berar (CP&B) state of British India which covered most of the central India. The riots occurred on 4 September 1927. On that day, there was a procession for Mahalakshmi, which is said to have been blocked by Muslims when it came to the Mahal neighborhood.

In the afternoon, there was rioting near the Hindu houses of the neighborhood, which continued for three days. The mutual trust between Hindu and Muslim communities had reached a low in the 1920s, and riots were seen frequently across many cities of India. In 1923, India witnessed eleven riots, in 1924 there were eighteen riots, in 1925 there were sixteen riots, and in 1926 there were thirty five riots. In the twelve months from May 1926 to April 1926, 40 more riots occurred across various cities.

They mostly occurred in Bengal, Punjab and United Provinces (UP). Lahore riots of August 1927 were the most deadly recorded riots in this series. The earlier riot of 1923 was caused when the members of Hindu Mahasabha took out a procession and passed in front of a mosque, playing loud music. The Muslim community objected, starting a skirmish between the two parties. These riots had a profound impact on K. B. Hedgewar, prompting him to form, in 1925, the Rashtriya Swayamsevak Sangh (RSS), a Hindu nationalist organization and one of the largest Hindu organizations in the world.

Christophe Jaffrelot in his book The Hindu Nationalist Movement and Indian Politics records a testimony saying that Hedgewar led the Ganesha procession in 1927, beating the drums in defiance of the usual practice not to pass in front of the mosque with music. All these events acted as a catalyst building up the tensions between two communities.

On the morning of 4 September, the day of Lakshmi Puja, Hindus took out a procession like every year, and passed in front of a mosque in the Mahal area of Nagpur. However, the Muslims stopped the procession this time around and did not allow it to pass through the area. In the afternoon, when the Hindus were resting after the morning procession, Muslim youths took out a procession shouting Allahu Akbar, armed with weapons like javelins, daggers and knives.

Muslim youths threw stones at the house of Hedgewar, who was then away from Nagpur. RSS cadres, sensing the mood of the procession, came out in the narrow lanes of the Mahal area and reciprocated with lathis, further intensifying the riots. Liaquat Ali Khan, in his book Pakistan – The Heart of Asia, also describes a major arson incident during the riot that seemed pre-meditated with explosives gathered well before the riots began.

The Washington Post reported 22 had been killed and more than 100 injured in riots that continued for two days. Later, the government ordered troops into the city to restore peace. During the riots, the RSS had grouped its cadres in 16 shakhas, spread out across the city to protect the Hindu communities.

RSS had showcased its role in defending Hindus during the riots. The popularity of the organization grew as the news of the incident spread across the country, and it saw a spurt in its membership. By 1929, the organization formed an elaborate hierarchical structure. Between 1931 and 1939, the number of its branches grew from 60 to 500. The membership count had reached 60,000 by this time.

1969 Gujarat Riots
The 1969 Gujarat riots refers to the communal violence between Hindus and Muslims during September–October 1969, in Gujarat, India. The violence was Gujarat's first major riot that involved massacre, arson and looting on a large scale. It was the most deadly Hindu-Muslim violence since the 1947 partition of India, and remained so until the 1989 Bhagalpur violence.

According to the official figures, 660 people were killed, 1074 people were injured and over 48,000 lost their property. Unofficial reports claim as high as 2000 deaths. The Muslim community suffered the majority of the losses. Out of the 512 deaths reported in the police complaints, 430 were Muslims. Property worth 42 million rupees was destroyed during the riots, with Muslims losing 32 million worth of property. A distinctive feature of the violence was the attack on Muslim chawls by their Dalit Hindu neighbors who had maintained peaceful relations with them until this point.

The riots happened during the chief ministership of the Indian National Congress leader Hitendra Desai. The Justice Reddy Commission set up by his government blamed the Hindu nationalist organizations for instigating the violence. Various writers trace the causes of the riots to a mix of socioeconomic and political factors. The violence started on 18 September 1969 after Muslims attacked some Hindu sadhus and a temple, after the cows herded by the sadhus caused injury to them. The Hindus later attacked a Muslim dargah, and Muslim protesters also attacked the temple again, leading to a mass breakout of violence. The riots started in Ahmedabad, and then spread to other areas, notably Vadodara, Mehsana, Nadiad, Anand and Gondal. By 26 September, the violence had been brought under control, however some more violent incidents happened during 18–28 October 1969.

The Hindu-Muslim tension increased considerably in Gujarat during the 1960s. Between 1961 and 1971, there were 685 incidents of communal violence in the urban areas of Gujarat (plus, another 114 in the rural areas). Out of the 685 incidents, 578 incidents happened in 1969 alone. Although Ahmedabad had been divided along the caste and religious lines, it was not a communally sensitive area until the 1960s.

In the 1960s, the city's textile mills attracted a large number of migrants from other parts of the state. During 1961-71, the city's population grew by nearly 38%, resulting in rapid growth of slums in the eastern part of the city. However, mid-1960s onwards, a number of under-qualified mill workers in Ahmedabad became unemployed, as the jobs went to the small units of Surat. During the 1960s, seven large mills in Ahmedabad shut down, and around 17,000 workers lost their jobs. The Hindus were over-represented among these workers, compared to the Muslims. The Dalit Hindu workers faced a greater sense of insecurity, as the local Muslim workers were said to be more skilled in the weaving.

Several violent clashes involving the textile workers took place in the slums of the city, mainly between the Hindu Dalits and the Muslims. The changing socioeconomic factors also impacted the political situation in the city. The Indian National Congress had been fragmenting, leading to tensions between its factions: the Congress eventually split into Congress (O) and Congress (I) in 1969. At the same time, the Hindu nationalist organization RSS had established local strongholds in the eastern parts of the city.

Several incidents led to increase in tensions between the two communities in Ahmedabad. During a three-day rally held in Maninagar during 27–28 December 1968, the RSS supremo M. S. Golwalkar pleaded for a Hindu Rashtra ("Hindu nation"). On the Muslim side, provocative speeches were made at the conference of Jamiat Ulema-e-Hind in June 1969.

On the evening of 3 March 1969, a Hindu police officer moved a handcart that was obstructing traffic near the Kalupur Tower. A copy of Koran placed on the handcart fell on the ground, resulting in a demand for an apology by a small Muslim crowd standing nearby. The crowd soon grew bigger, and twelve policemen were injured in the subsequent violent protests. On 31 August, the Muslims of the city held a massive demonstration to protest the burning of the Al-Aqsa Mosque in Jerusalem.

On 4 September, a Muslim sub-inspector, while dispersing a Ramlila festive crowd, hit a table. As a result, the Hindu text Ramayana and an Aarti thali (plate) fell down. The Hindus alleged that the police officer also kicked the sacred book. This incident led to protests by Hindus, and the formation of the Hindu Dharma Raksha Samiti by the RSS leaders. The Hindu Dharma Raksha Samiti ("Hindu Religion Protection Committee") organized protests in which anti-Muslim slogans were raised. The Bharatiya Jana Sangh leader Balraj Madhok visited the city and made fiery speeches on 14 and 15 September. Another incident included an alleged assault on some Muslim maulvis, who were trying to construct a mosque in the Odhav village near Ahmedabad.

On 18 September 1969, a Muslim crowd had gathered in the Jamalpur area of Ahmedabad to celebrate the local Urs festival at the tomb of a Sufi saint (Bukhari Saheb's Chilla). When the sadhus (Hindu holy men) of the nearby Jagannath temple tried to bring their cows back to the temple compound through the crowded streets, some Muslim women were injured. The cows also allegedly damaged some carts on which the Muslims were selling goods. This led to violence in which some Muslim youths attacked and injured the sadhus, and damaged the temple windows. Sevadasji, the mahant (priest) of the Hindu temple, went on a protest fast, which he gave up after a 15-member Muslim delegation led by A.M. Peerzada met him and apologized.

However, subsequently, a dargah (tomb shrine) near the temple was damaged by some Hindus. A large number of Muslims protestors gathered in the area. On the afternoon of 19 September, a crowd of 2500-3000 Muslims attacked the temple again. Following this, the rumors spread and the violence escalated, resulting in several incidents of arson, murders and attacks on the places of worship around the area. The Muslims in the eastern areas of the city and its suburbs started fleeing their homes for safer areas. Several trains carrying them were stopped and attacked. A curfew was imposed on the evening of 19 September, and on the next day, the army was called in to control the violence.

During 19–24 September, 514 people were killed. This period also saw damage to 6,123 houses and shops, mainly by Hindus. In the afternoon of 20 September 1969, a young Muslim man, angry at the destruction of his property by Hindus, announced that he would take revenge. An angry Hindu mob beat him up and asked him to shout Jai Jagannath ("Hail Jagannath"). The Muslim man said that he would rather die. The crowd then sprinkled petrol on him and burnt him to death. The municipal corporation by-election scheduled for 22 September was postponed. The first curfew relaxation on the next day resulted in 30 deaths within the first 3 hours.

After a year of time, according to the Justice Reddy Commission set up by the Congress Government to investigate the riots, the Hindu nationalist organizations like RSS, Hindu Mahasabha and Jan Sangh were involved in the riots. The Justice Jaganmohan Reddy Commission of Enquiry was set up by the Government of Gujarat's Home Department. It published a seventeen page report in the year of 1971, questioning the police's role in the riots.

It found around six instances of Muslim religious places adjoining police lines or police stations being attacked or damaged. The police defended themselves claiming these police stations did not have adequate strength since the forces were busy quelling the riots at other places. This kind of excuses is common in India. However, the commission refused to entertain this argument, since there was no report of damage to a Hindu place of worship near any police station. This violence created a lot of destructions. According to an overall record, 37 mosques, 50 dargahs, 6 kabristans (Muslim graveyards) and 3 temples were destroyed.

The journalist Ajit Bhattacharjea accused the police of not taking any "firm action for the first three days", and stated that "this was not a matter of slackness but policy". An unnamed senior Congress leader told him that their government was reluctant to use force because it was afraid of losing power to Jan Sangh in the next elections in case it did so.

The Bharatiya Janta Party, which was called Bharatiya Jana Sangh at that time, had strong hold in Gujrat among Hindu community. They had their head office in Gandhinagar for the statewide political operation. As they were the part of Rashtriya Swemsewak Sangh (RSS), so they were getting benefits of Hindutva. The members of the Bharatiya Jana Sangh called the violence a revenge for the massacre of Hindus by the Muslim League in 1946.

On 26 September, a Hindu organization called Sangram Samiti claimed that the Congress-led government had been appeasing the Muslims, and had been encouraging the "abolition of Hindu religion under the name of secularism". The Hindu organizations claimed that after the alleged desecration of the Koran in March, the Hindu police officer had to apologize twice, while "it took days for taking any steps when the Hindus were similarly insulted" after the alleged desecration of the Ramayana in September.

According to the author and social activist Achyut Yagnik, the 1969 riots were a turning point in the Hindu-Muslim relations in Gujarat, and led to a drop in the tolerance levels, which was visible in the later riots of 1992-93 and 2002. After the 1969 riots, the state saw increasing Muslim ghettoization.

This ferocity was explained differently by media for political means. The Times of India, Asian Age and other newspapers highlighted the issue. According to the Hindustan Times report in 2011, the violence was "deliberately engineered" to discredit the chief minister Hitendra Desai, who had been supporting the Congress (O) leader Morarji Desai instead of the Congress (I) leader Indira Gandhi.

Chapter 9
1984 Anti-Sikh Riots

The 1984 anti-Sikh riots, also known as the 1984 Sikh Massacre, was a series of organized pogroms against Sikhs in India in response to the assassination of Indira Gandhi by her Sikh bodyguards. The ruling Indian National Congress had been in active complicity with the mob, as to the organization of the riots. Government estimates project that about 2,800 Sikhs were killed in Delhi and 3,350 nationwide, whilst independent sources estimate the number of deaths at about 8,000–17,000.

The violence continued in the early 1980s in Punjab because of the armed Sikh separatist Khalistan movement which sought independence from India. In July 1982, the Sikh political party Akali Dal's President Harchand Singh Longowal had invited Jarnail Singh Bhindranwale to take up residence in Golden Temple Complex to evade arrest.

Jarnail Singh Bhindranwale later on made the sacred temple complex an armory and headquarters for his separatist movement of Punjab. In the violent events leading up to the Operation Blue Star since the inception of Akali Dharm Yudh Morcha, the militants had killed 165 Hindus and Nirankaris, even 39 Sikhs opposed to Bhindranwale were killed. The total number of deaths was 410 in violent incidents and riots while 1,180 people were injured. Operation Blue Star was an Indian military operation carried out between 1 and 8 June 1984, ordered by Prime Minister Indira Gandhi to remove militant religious leader Jarnail Singh Bhindranwale and his armed militants from the buildings of the Harmandir Sahib complex in Amritsar, Punjab.

Bhindranwale died and militants were removed from the temple complex. The military action in the temple complex was criticized by Sikhs worldwide who had interpreted it as an assault on Sikh religion. Four months after the operation, on 31 October 1984, Indira Gandhi was assassinated in vengeance by her two Sikh bodyguards, Satwant Singh and Beant Singh, who shot Indira Gandhi 33 times.

Public outcry over Gandhi's death led to the killings of Sikhs in the ensuing riots. In the aftermath of the riots, the government reported that 20,000 had fled the city; the People's Union for Civil Liberties reported "at least" 1,000 displaced persons. The most-affected regions were the Sikh neighborhoods of Delhi. Human rights organizations and newspapers across India believed that the massacre was organized. The collusion of political officials in the violence and judicial failure to penalize the perpetrators alienated Sikhs and increased support for the Khalistan movement. The Akal Takht, Sikhism's governing body, considers the killings genocide.

In 2011, Human Rights Watch reported that the Government of India had "yet to prosecute those responsible for the mass killings". According to the 2011 WikiLeaks cable leaks, the United States was convinced of Indian National Congress' complicity in the riots and called it "opportunism" and "hatred" by the Congress government, of Sikhs. Although the U.S. has not identified the riots as genocide, it acknowledged that "grave human rights violations" occurred.

In 2011, a new group of mass graves was discovered in Haryana and Human Rights Watch reported that "widespread anti-Sikh attacks in Haryana were part of broader revenge attacks" in India.The Central Bureau of Investigation, the main Indian investigative agency, believes that the violence was organized with support from the Delhi police and some central-government officials.

In 1972 Punjab state elections, Congress won and Akali Dal was defeated. In 1973, Akali Dal put forward the Anandpur Sahib Resolution to demand more autonomy to Punjab. It demanded that power be generally given from the Central to state governments. The Congress government considered the resolution a secessionist document and rejected it. Bhindranwale then joined the Akali Dal to launch the Dharam Yudh Morcha in 1982 to implement the Anandpur Sahib resolution.

Bhindranwale had risen to prominence in the Sikh political circle with his policy of getting the Anandpur Resolution passed, failing which he wanted to declare a separate country of Khalistan as a homeland for Sikhs. Others demanded an autonomous state in India, based on the Anandpur Sahib Resolution. Many Sikhs condemned the militants' actions.

Bhindranwale symbolized the revivalist, extremist and terrorist movement in the 1980s in Punjab. He is credited with launching the Sikh militancy in Punjab. Under him, number of people initiated into the Khalsa increased. He also increased the level of rhetoric on the perceived "assault" on Sikh values from the Hindu community. He and his followers started carrying firearms at all times. In 1983, to escape arrest, he along with his militant cadre occupied and fortified the Sikh shrine Akal Takht. By 1983, the situation in Punjab was volatile. In October, Sikh militants stopped a bus and shot six Hindu passengers. On the same day, another group killed two officials on a train. The Congress-led central government dismissed the Punjab state government (led by their party), invoking the president's rule in the state.

During the five months before Operation Blue Star, from 1 January to 3 June 1984, 298 people were killed in violent incidents across Punjab. In the five days preceding the operation, 48 people were killed by violence. In the violent events leading up to the Operation Blue Star since the inception of Akali Dharm Yudh Morcha, the militants had killed 165 Hindus and Nirankaris, and even 39 Sikhs opposed to Bhindranwale were killed. The total number of deaths was 410 in violent incidents and riots while 1,180 people were injured.

On 1 June, Operation Blue Star was launched to remove him and the armed militants from the Golden Temple complex. On 6 June Bhindranwale died in the operation. Casualty figures for the Army were 83 dead and 249 injured. According to the official estimate presented by the Indian government, 1592 were apprehended and there were 493 combined militant and civilian casualties. High civilian casualties were attributed to militants using pilgrims trapped inside the temple as human shields. Later operations by Indian paramilitary forces were conducted to clear the separatists from the state of Punjab.

The operation carried out in the temple caused outrage among the Sikhs and increased the support for Khalistan Movement. Four months after the operation, on 31 October 1984, Indira Gandhi was assassinated in vengeance by her two Sikh bodyguards, Satwant Singh and Beant Singh. One of the assassins was fatally shot by Gandhi's other bodyguards while the other was convicted of Gandhi's murder and then executed. Public outcry over Gandhi's death led to the killings of Sikhs in the riots.

After the assassination of Indira Gandhi on 31 October 1984 by two of her Sikh bodyguards, anti-Sikh riots erupted the following day. They continued in some areas for several days, killing more than 3,000 Sikhs in New Delhi and an estimated 8,000 – 17,000 or more Sikhs were killed in 40 cities across India. At least 50,000 Sikhs were displaced. Sultanpuri, Mangolpuri, Trilokpuri, and other Trans-Yamuna areas of Delhi were the worst affected.

Perpetrators carried iron rods, knives, clubs, and combustible material (including kerosene and petrol). They entered Sikh neighborhoods, killing Sikhs indiscriminately and destroying shops and houses. Armed mobs stopped buses and trains in and near Delhi, pulling off Sikh passengers for lynching; some were burnt alive. Others were dragged from their homes and hacked to death, and Sikh women were reportedly gang-raped and Sikhs also had acid thrown on them.

Such wide-scale violence cannot take place without police help. Delhi Police, whose paramount duty was to upkeep law and order situation and protect innocent lives, gave full help to rioters who were in fact working under able guidance of sycophant leaders like Jagdish Tytler and H K L Bhagat. It is a known fact that many jails, sub-jails and lock-ups were opened for three days and prisoners, for the most part hardened criminals, were provided fullest provisions, means and instruction to "teach the Sikhs a lesson". But it will be wrong to say that Delhi Police did nothing, for it took full and keen action against Sikhs who tried to defend themselves.

The Sikhs who opened fire to save their lives and property had to spend months dragging heels in courts after-wards. The riots have also been described as pogroms, massacres or genocide. On 31 October, a crowd around the All India Institute of Medical Sciences began shouting vengeance slogans such as "Blood for blood!" and became an unruly mob. At 17:20, President Zail Singh arrived at the hospital and the mob stoned his car. It began assaulting Sikhs, stopping cars and buses to pull Sikhs out and burn them.

The violence on 31 October, restricted to the area around the AIIMS, resulted in many Sikh deaths. Residents of other parts of Delhi reported that their neighborhoods were peaceful. During the night of 31 October and the morning of 1 November, Congress Party leaders met with local supporters to distribute money and weapons. Congress MP Sajjan Kumar and trade-union leader Lalit Maken handed out rupees 100 notes and bottles of liquor to the assailants. On the morning of 1 November, Sajjan Kumar was observed holding rallies in the Delhi neighborhoods of Palam Colony (from 06:30 to 07:00), Kiran Gardens (08:00 to 08:30), and Sultanpuri (about 08:30 to 09:00).

In Kiran Gardens at 8:00 am, Kumar was observed distributing iron rods from a parked truck to a group of 120 people and ordering them to "attack Sikhs, kill them, and loot and burn their properties". During the morning he led a mob along the Palam railway road to Mangolpuri, where the crowd chanted: "Kill the Sardars" and "Indira Gandhi is our mother and these people have killed her". In Sultanpuri, Moti Singh (a Sikh Congress Party member for 20 years) heard Kumar make the following speech:

Whoever kills the sons of the snakes, I will reward them. Whoever kills Roshan Singh and Bagh Singh will get 5,000 rupees each and 1,000 rupees each for killing any other Sikhs. You can collect these prizes on November 3 from my personal assistant Jai Chand Jamadar. The Central Bureau of Investigation told the court that during the riot, Kumar said that "not a single Sikh should survive". The bureau accused Delhi police of keeping its "eyes closed" during the riot, which was planned.

In the Shakarpur neighborhood, Congress Party leader Shyam Tyagi's home was used as a meeting place for an undetermined number of people. Minister of Information and Broadcasting H. K. L. Bhagat gave money to Boop Tyagi (Tyagi's brother), saying: "Keep these two thousand rupees for liquor and do as I have told you ... You need not worry at all. I will look after everything."

During the night of 31 October, Balwan Khokhar (a local Congress Party leader who was implicated in the massacre) held a meeting at Pandit Harkesh's ration shop in Palam. Congress Party supporter Shankar Lal Sharma held a meeting, where he assembled a mob which swore to kill Sikhs, in his shop at 08:30 on 1 November.

Kerosene, the primary mob weapon, was supplied by a group of Congress Party leaders who owned filling stations. In Sultanpuri, Congress Party A-4 block president Brahmanand Gupta distributed oil while Sajjan Kumar "instructed the crowd to kill Sikhs, and to loot and burn their properties" (as he had done at other meetings throughout New Delhi). Similar meetings were held at locations such as Cooperative Colony in Bokaro, where local Congress president and gas-station owner P. K. Tripathi distributed kerosene to mobs.

Aseem Shrivastava, a graduate student at the Delhi School of Economics, described the mobs' organized nature in an affidavit submitted to the Misra Commission:

The attack on Sikhs and their property in our locality appeared to be an extremely organized affair ... There were also some young men on motorcycles, who were instructing the mobs and supplying them with kerosene oil from time to time. On more than a few occasions we saw auto-rickshaw arriving with several tins of kerosene oil and other inflammable material, such as jute sacks.

A senior official at the Ministry of Home Affairs told journalist Ivan Fera that an arson investigation of several businesses burned in the riots had found an unnamed combustible chemical "whose provision required large-scale coordination". Eyewitness reports confirmed the use of a combustible chemical in addition to kerosene. The Delhi Sikh Gurdwara Management Committee later cited 70 affidavits noting the use of a highly-flammable chemical in its written reports to the Misra Commission.

On 31 October, Congress Party officials provided assailants with voter lists, school registration forms, and ration lists. The lists were used to find Sikh homes and business, an otherwise-impossible task because they were in unmarked, diverse neighborhoods. During the night of 31 October, before the massacres began, assailants used the lists to mark Sikh houses with an "S". Because most mob members were illiterate, Congress Party officials provided help reading the lists and leading the mobs to Sikh homes and businesses. With the lists, the mobs could pinpoint the location of Sikhs they otherwise would have missed. Sikh men not at home were easily identified by their turbans and beards, and Sikh women were identified by their dress. In some cases, the mobs returned to locations where they knew Sikhs were hiding because of the lists. Amar Singh escaped the initial attack on his house by having a Hindu neighbor drag him into the neighbor's house and announce that he was dead.

A group of 18 assailants later came looking for his body; when his neighbor said that his body had been taken away, an assailant showed him a list and said: "Look, Amar Singh's name has not been struck off from the list, so his body has not been taken away." The Delhi High Court, delivering its verdict on a riot-related case in 2009, said, "Though we boast of being the world's largest democracy and the Delhi being its national capital, the sheer mention of the incidents of 1984 anti-Sikh riots in general and the role played by Delhi Police and state machinery in particular makes our heads hang in shame in the eyes of the world polity."

The government allegedly destroyed evidence and shielded the guilty people involved in the massacre. The incident was criticized by some newspapers and radio channels, but not all. One of the newspapers of the capital, the Asian Age, an Indian daily newspaper, ran a front-page story calling the government actions "the mother of all cover-ups".

From 31 October 1984 to 10 November 1984 the People's Union for Democratic Rights and the People's Union for Civil Liberties conducted an inquiry into the riots, interviewing victims, police officers, neighbors of the victims, army personnel and political leaders. In their joint report, "Who Are The Guilty", the groups concluded:

The attacks on members of the Sikh Community in Delhi and its suburbs during the period, far from being a spontaneous expression of "madness" and of popular "grief and anger" at Mrs. Gandhi's assassination as made out to be by the authorities, were the outcome of a well-organized plan marked by acts of both deliberate commissions and omissions by important politicians of the Congress (I) at the top and by authorities in the administration.

According to eyewitness accounts obtained by Time magazine, Delhi police looked on as "rioters murdered and raped, having gotten access to voter records that allowed them to mark Sikh homes with large Xs, and large mobs being bused in to large Sikh settlements". Time reported that the riots led to only minor arrests, with no major politicians or police officers convicted. The magazine quoted Ensaaf, an Indian human-rights organization, as saying that the government attempted to destroy evidence of its involvement by refusing to record First Information Reports.

A 1991 Human Rights Watch report on violence between Sikh separatists and the Government of India traced part of the problem to government response to the violence: Despite numerous credible eye-witness accounts that identified many of those involved in the violence, including police and politicians, in the months following the killings, the government sought no prosecutions or indictments of any persons, including officials, accused in any case of murder, rape or arson. The violence was allegedly led (and often perpetrated) by Indian National Congress activists and sympathizers. The Congress-led government was widely criticized for doing little at the time and possibly conspiring in the riots, since voter lists were used to identify Sikh families.

A few days after the massacre, many surviving Sikh youths in Delhi had joined or created Sikh militant groups. This led to more violence in Punjab, including the assassination of several senior Congress Party members. The Khalistan Commando Force and Khalistan Liberation Force claimed responsibility for the retaliation, and an underground network was established.

On 31 July 1985, Harjinder Singh Jinda, Sukhdev Singh Sukha and Ranjit Singh Gill of the Khalistan Commando Force assassinated Congress Party leader and MP Lalit Maken in retaliation for the riots. The 31-page report, "Who Are The Guilty?" listed 227 people who led the mobs; Maken was third on the list.

Harjinder Jinda and Sukhdev Singh Sukha assassinated Congress Party leader Arjan Dass because of his involvement in the riots. Dass' name appeared in affidavits submitted by Sikh victims to the Nanavati Commission, headed by retired Supreme Court judge Nanavati. In Delhi, 442 rioters were convicted. Forty-nine were sentenced to the life imprisonment, and another three to more than 10 years' imprisonment. Six Delhi police officers were sanctioned for negligence during the riots. In April 2013, the Supreme Court of India dismissed the appeal of three people who had challenged their life sentences. That month, the Karkardooma district court in Delhi convicted five people – Balwan Khokkar (former councilor), Mahender Yadav (former MLA), Kishan Khokkar, Girdhari Lal and Captain Bhagmal – for inciting a mob against Sikhs in Delhi Cantonment. The court acquitted Congress leader Sajjan Kumar, which led to protests.

In the first ever case of capital punishment in the 1984 anti-Sikh riots case death sentence was awarded to Yashpal Singh convicted for murdering two persons, 24-year-old Hardev Singh and 26-year-old Avtar Singh, in Mahipal Pur area of Delhi on 1 November 1984. Additional Sessions Judge Ajay Pandey pronounced the Judgment on 20 November 34 years after the crime was committed. The second convict in the case, Naresh Sehrawat was awarded life imprisonment. The Court considered the failing health of 68-year-old Sehrawat while giving him a lighter sentence. The conviction followed a complaint by the deceased Hardev Singh's elder brother Santokh Singh.

Though an FIR was filed on the same day of the crime nothing came of the case as a Congress leader, JP Singh, who led the mob was acquitted in the case. A fresh FIR was filed on 29 April 1993, following recommendations of the Ranganath Commission of inquiry. The police closed the matter as untraced despite witness testimonies of the deceased's four brothers who were witness to the crime. The case was reopened by the Special Investigation Team constituted by the BJP-led NDA government on 12 February 2015. The SIT completed the investigation in record time. The first conviction resulting from the formation of the SIT came on 15 November 2018, by the conviction of Naresh Sehrawat and Yashpal Singh. Subsequently, one of the first high-profile conviction of Sajjan Kumar by Delhi High Court who was earlier acquitted by the lower court on 17 December 2018.

Chapter 10
1989 Insurgency in Kashmir

The Kashmir insurgency is an uprising or revolt against the Indian administration of Jammu and Kashmir, a region constituting the southern portion of the larger Kashmir region, which was the subject of a dispute between India and Pakistan since 1947.

Looking into the reason of uprising, we come to the fact that Jammu and Kashmir, long a breeding ground of separatist ambitions, has been wracked by the insurgency since 1989. Although the failure of Indian governance and democracy lay at the root of the initial disaffection, Pakistan played an important role in converting the latter into a fully developed insurgency.

Some insurgent groups in Kashmir support the complete independence, whereas others seek accession to Pakistan. More explicitly, the roots of the insurgency are tied to a dispute over local autonomy. Democratic development was limited in Kashmir until the late 1970s and by 1988 many of the democratic reforms provided by the Indian government had been reversed and non-violent channels for expressing discontent were limited and caused a dramatic increase in support for insurgents advocating violent secession from India.

In 1987, a disputed State election created a catalyst for the uprising when it resulted in some of the state's legislative assembly members forming armed rebellious groups. In July 1988, a series of demonstrations, strikes and attacks on the Indian government began the Kashmir insurgency, which during the 1990s escalated into the most important internal security issue in India.

Pakistan claims to be giving its "moral and diplomatic" support to the separatist movement. The Inter-Services Intelligence of Pakistan has been accused by India and the international community of supporting, supplying arms and training mujahideen, to fight in Jammu and Kashmir. In 2015, former President of Pakistan Pervez Musharraf admitted that Pakistan had supported and trained insurgent groups in the 1990s.

India has repeatedly called Pakistan to end its "cross-border terrorism" in Kashmir. Several new militant groups with radical Islamic views emerged and changed the ideological emphasis of the movement to Islamic. This had happened partly due to a large number of Islamic "Jihadi" fighters (mujahadeen) who had entered the Kashmir valley following the end of the Soviet–Afghan War in the 1980s.

The conflict between the militants and the Indian forces have led to large number of casualties. Many civilians have also died as a result of being targeted by the various armed groups. According to official figures released in Jammu and Kashmir assembly, there were 3,400 disappearance cases and the conflict has left more than 47,000 people dead which also includes 7,000 police personnel as of July 2009. However, the number of insurgency-related deaths in the state have fallen sharply since the start of a slow-moving peace process between India and Pakistan. Some rights groups claim a higher figure of 100,000 deaths since 1989.

After independence from colonial rule India and Pakistan fought a war over the princely state of Kashmir. At the end of the war India controlled the most valuable parts of Kashmir. While there were sporadic periods of violence there was no organized revolt movement. During this period legislative elections in Jammu and Kashmir were first held in 1951 and Sheikh Abdullah's secular party stood unopposed. He was an instrumental member in the accession of the state to India.

However Sheikh Abdullah would fall in and out of favor with the central government and would often be dismissed only to be re-appointed later on. This was a time of political instability & power struggle in Jammu and Kashmir and it went through several periods of President's rule by the Federal Government. After Sheikh Abdullah's death, his son Farooq Abdullah took over as Chief Minister of Jammu and Kashmir.

Farooq Abdullah eventually fell out of favor with the Central Government and the Prime Minister Indira Gandhi had his government toppled with the help of his brother-in-law G. M. Shah. A year later, Abdullah reached an accord with the new Prime Minister Rajiv Gandhi and announced an alliance with the Congress party for the elections of 1987. The elections were allegedly rigged in favor of Abdullah.

Most commentators state that this led to the rise of an armed insurgency movement composed, in part, of those who unfairly lost the elections. Pakistan supplied these groups with logistical support, arms, recruits and training. In the second half of 1989 the alleged assassinations of the Indian spies and political collaborators by JKLF (Jammu and Kashmir Liberation Front) was intensified. Over six months, more than a hundred officials were killed to paralyses government's administrative and intelligence apparatus.

The daughter of then interior affairs minister, Mufti Mohammad Sayeed was kidnapped in December and four terrorists had to be released for her release. This event led to mass celebrations all over the valley. Farooq Abdullah resigned in January after the appointment of Jagmohan Malhotra as the Governor of Jammu and Kashmir. Subsequently, J&K was placed under Governor's Rule under Article 92 of state constitution.

Under JKLF's leadership on January 21–23 large scale protests were organized in valley. As a response to this largely explosive situation paramilitary units of BSF and CRPF were called. These units were used by the government to combat Maoist and North-Eastern rebellions. The challenge to them in this situation was not posed by armed insurgents but by the stone palters. Their inexperience caused at least 50 casualties in Gawkadal massacre. In this incident the underground militant movement was transformed into a mass struggle. To curb the situation AFSPA (Armed Forces Special Powers Act) was imposed on Kashmir in September 1990 to suppress the radical movement by giving armed forces the powers to kill and arrest without warrant to maintain public order.

During this time the dominant tactic involved killing of a prominent figure in a public gathering to push forces into action and the public prevented them from capturing these insurgents. This sprouting of sympathizers in Kashmir led to the hardline approach of Indian army.

With JKLF at forefront large number of militant groups like Allah Tigers, People's League and Hizb-i-Islamia sprung up. Weapons were smuggled on a large scale from Pakistan. In Kashmir, JKLF operated under the leadership of Ashfaq Majid Wani, Yasin Bhat, Hamid Shiekh and Javed Mir.

To counter this growing pro-Pakistani sentiment in the Kashmir region, Indian media associated it exclusively with Pakistan. JKLF militant force used distinctly Islamic themes to mobilize crowds and justify their use of violence. They sought to establish an Islamic democratic state where the rights of minorities would be protected according to Quran and Sunna and economy would be organized on the principles of Islamic socialism. The Indian army has conducted various operations to control and eliminate insurgency in the region such as Operation Sarp Vinash, in which a multi-battalion offensive was launched against terrorists from groups like Lashkar-e-Taiba, Harkat-ul-Jihad-e-Islami, al-Badr and Jaish-e-Mohammad who had been constructing shelters in the Pir Panjal region of Jammu and Kashmir over several years.

The subsequent operations led to the death of over 60 terrorists and uncovered the largest network of militant hideouts in the history of Jammu and Kashmir covering 100 square kilometers. During the early period of militancy in 1989, multiple militants groups strive to Islamize Kashmiri culture and political setup to create a conducive environment for the merger of Kashmir with Pakistan. Numerous Islamist groups were formed in early 1990 who emerged advocating Nizam-e-Mustafa (Rule of Muhammad) as the objective for their struggle. Militant groups like Hizbul mujahideen and Jamaat-e-Islami asserted that struggle of Kashmir will continue till Islamic Caliphate is achieved in Kashmir. Murder of Kashmiri Hindus, Intellectuals, Liberals and activists were described necessary to get rid of un-Islamic elements.

Concurrently all cinema houses, beauty parlors, wine shops, dance bars, video centers, use of cosmetics and similar things were banned by militant groups. Many militant organizations like Al baqr, People's league, Wahdat-e-Islam and Allah Tigers imposed restrictions like banning cigarettes, restrictions on Kashmiri girls.

Apart from militants, Kashmir was witnessing Islamization during 1980's when Abdullah Government changed the names of about 2,500 villages from their native names to new Islamic names. The Sheikh also started delivering communal speeches in mosques similar to his speeches in the 1930s. Additionally, he referred Kashmiri Pandits as "mukhbir" or informers of the Indian government.

The Afghan jihad against the Soviets, the Islamic Revolution in Iran, and the armed struggle of the Sikhs in Punjab against the Indian state became sources of inspiration for large numbers of Kashmiri Muslim youth. Both the pro-Independence JKLF and the pro-Pakistan Islamist groups including Jamaat-e-Islami Kashmir mobilized the fast growing anti-Indian sentiments among the Kashmiri population. The year of 1984 saw a pronounced rise in terrorist violence in Kashmir. When the JKLF militant Maqbool Bhat was executed in February 1984, strikes and protests by Kashmiri nationalists broke out in the region, where large number of Kashmiri youth participated in widespread anti-India demonstrations, which faced heavy handed reprisals by the state forces.

The Hindus of the Kashmir Valley, were forced to flee the Kashmir valley as a result of being targeted by JKLF and Islamist insurgents during late 1989 and early 1990. Of the approximately 300,000 to 600,000 Hindus living in the Kashmir Valley in 1990 only 2,000–3,000 remain there in 2016. January 19, 1990 is widely remembered by Kashmiri Hindus as the tragic "exodus day" of being forced out of Kashmir. According to the Indian government, more than 62,000 families are registered as Kashmiri refugees including some Sikh and Muslim families. Most families were resettled in Jammu, National Capital Region surrounding Delhi and other neighboring states.

Under the 1975 accord, Sheikh Abdullah agreed to measures previously undertaken by the central government in Jammu and Kashmir to integrate the state into India. Sociologist Farrukh Faheem states that it was met with hostility among people of Kashmir and laid the groundwork for the future uproar in the state. Those opposed to it included Jamaat-e-Islami Kashmir and People's League in Indian Jammu and Kashmir, and Jammu Kashmir Liberation Front (JKLF) based in Azad Kashmir. Since the mid-1970s, communalist rhetoric was being exploited in the state for vote-bank politics. Pakistan's Inter-Services Intelligence (ISI) tried to spread Wahhabism in place of Sufism to foster religious unity with their nation, the communalization helped in furthering it.

February 1986, Gul Shah on his return to Kashmir valley retaliated and incited the Kashmiri Muslims by saying Islam is in danger. As a result, Kashmiri Hindus were targeted by the Kashmiri Muslims. Many incidents were reported in various areas where Kashmiri Hindus were killed and their properties and temples damaged or destroyed. The worst hit areas were mainly in South Kashmir.

During the Anantnag riot in February 1986, although no Hindu was killed, many houses and other properties belonging to Hindus were looted, burnt or damaged. An investigation of Anantnag riots revealed that members of the 'secular parties' in the state, rather than the Islamists, had played a key role in organizing the violence to gain political mileage through religious sentiments. Shah called in the army to curb the violence, but it had little effect. His government was dismissed on 12 March 1986, by the then Governor Jagmohan following communal riots in south Kashmir.

This led Jagmohan to rule the state directly. The political fight was hence being portrayed as a conflict between "Hindu" New Delhi (Central Government), and its efforts to impose its will in the state, and "Muslim" Kashmir, represented by political Islamists and clerics. Islamists had organized under a banner named Muslim United Front, with manifesto to work for Islamic unity and against political interference from the center, and contested the 1987 state elections, in which they lost again.

However, the 1987 elections were widely believed to be rigged so as to bring the secular parties in Kashmir at the forefront, and this caused the insurgency in Kashmir. The Kashmiri militants killed anyone who openly expressed pro-India policies. Kashmiri Hindus were targeted specifically because they were seen as presenting Indian presence in Kashmir because of their faith.

Though the insurgency had been launched by JKLF, groups rose over the next few months advocating for establishment of Nizam-e-Mustafa (Rule of Muhammad). The Islamist groups proclaimed the Islamicization of socio-political and economic set-up, merger with Pakistan, unification of ummah and establishment of an Islamic Caliphate.

Liquidation of central government officials, Hindus, liberal and nationalist intellectuals, social and cultural activists was described as necessary to rid the valley of un-Islamic elements. The relations among the semi-secular and Islamists groups were generally poor and often hostile. The JKLF had also utilized Islamic formulations in its mobilization strategies and public discourse, using Islam and independence interchangeably. It demanded equal rights for everyone however this had a distinct Islamic flavor as it sought to establish an Islamic democracy, protection of minority rights per Quran and Sunnah and an economy of Islamic socialism. The pro-separatist political practices at times deviated from their stated secular position.

The JKLF group targeted a Kashmiri Hindu for the first time on 14 September 1989, when they killed Tika Lal Taploo, an advocate and a prominent leader of Bharatiya Janata Party in Jammu & Kashmir in front of several eyewitnesses. This instilled fear in the Kashmiri Hindus especially as Taploo's killers were never caught which also emboldened the terrorists.

The Hindus felt that they weren't safe in the valley and could be targeted any time. The killings of Kashmiri Hindus continued that included many of the prominent ones. In order to undermine his political rival, Farooq Abdullah who at that time was the Chief Minister of Jammu and Kashmir, the Minister of Home Affairs Mufti Mohammad Sayeed convinced Prime Minister V.P. Singh to appoint Jagmohan as the governor of the state. Abdullah resented Jagmohan who had been appointed as the governor earlier in April 1984 as well and had recommended Abdullah's dismissal to Rajiv Gandhi in July 1984. Abdullah had earlier declared that he would resign if Jagmohan was made the Governor. However, the Central government went ahead and appointed him as Governor on 19 January 1990. In response, Abdullah resigned on the same day and Jagmohan suggested the dissolution of the State Assembly.

Chapter 11
Ayodhya Firing Incident

Uttar Pradesh state of India started facing turbulence since 1990. The center of Hindu uprising was the Ram Janmabhoomi of Ayodhya. The Ayodhya firing incident describes the occasion when the Uttar Pradesh police fired live ammunition at civilians on two separate days, 30 October 1990 and 2 November 1990. The civilians were religious Hindu volunteers, assembled near the Ram Janmabhoomi site at Ayodhya. The state government's official records report that 16 people were killed.

In September 1990, around thirty years from today, the Vishwa Hindu Parishad (VHP), the Rashtriya Swayamsevak Sangh (RSS) and the Bhartiya Janata Party campaigned for a new Ram Temple to be built at the Ram Janmabhoomi site. The situation became volatile, with L. K. Advani conducting rath yatra and the VHP mobilizing people to the site. The state government, under Mulayam Singh Yadav, promised protection and a complete lockdown of the site and city. Yadav reassured the public: "No bird would be able to fly into Ayodhya".

The Hindu volunteers first assembled in Ayodhya, at the behest of L. K. Advani of the BJP and Ashok Singhal of the VHP, on 21 October 1990. Just two weeks later, 30 October saw the start of unprecedented security arrangements in the state. Police barred all bus and train services to Ayodhya. Most volunteers reached Ayodhya by foot; some swam across the Sarayu River.

The police also barricaded the 1.5 km-long climb to the disputed structure and imposed a curfew. According to the investigatory Liberhan Commission report, issued after the event:

28,000 Uttar Pradesh Provincial Armed Constabulary personnel were deployed in Ayodhya.
Out of 40,000 volunteers, only 10,000 managed to reach Ayodhya.
At around 10 am, a large group of volunteers headed towards the site.

The large group was led by Vamadev, Mahant Nratyagopal Das, and Ashok Singhal of the VHP. Ashok Singhal was wounded on the head by a police baton. This altercation led to a mob frenzy and open confrontation between civilians and policemen. At around 11 am, a Hindu holy-man or sadhu managed to gain control of an Armed Constabulary bus in which the police were holding detainees. The sadhu drove the bus right through the barricades, clearing a way for the others to follow on foot. The security forces were caught off guard and were forced to chase about 5,000 volunteers, who stormed through the heavily guarded site.

According to eyewitnesses the Kothari brothers mounted a saffron flag atop the Babri Masjid. On the orders of Mulayam Government, security personnel fired on the crowd and chased volunteers across the area. Many people died from head wounds. There was a stampede at the Saryu Bridge, which killed a number of people.

Hindu groups took a day of rest on 1 November. On 2 November 1990, they offered prayers at Ramlila in the morning and then proceeded to Babri Masjid. Members of the crowd used the strategy of touching security personnel's feet, which made them withdraw a step. This worked for a while, and the procession continued. However, the police took firm action by using tear gas and baton charges to disperse the crowd. Nevertheless, some contingents of volunteers reached and partially damaged the mosque.

In response, the police opened fire for the second time in 72 hours, and chased them through the alleys around Hanumangarhi. In one place, later named Shaheed Gali or Martyr's Alley, police killed many of them – this included the Kothari Brothers, who were allegedly dragged out of a mosque. Some liberal Indians have accused the police of disposing of many dead bodies, either by cremating them at unknown places or by dumping them into the Saryu River in sacks. News of the shootings was mostly suppressed from the Indian media, but some local and international media outlets mentioned them on their channels.

The firing incident had a major impact on Uttar Pradesh and on Indian national politics. The Chief Minister of Uttar Pradesh was given the sobriquet 'Mulla' Mulayam Singh for his pro-Muslim stance during the incident. He lost the 1991 election to the Bhartiya Janata Party. He described his decision to fire on the crowd in Ayodhya as "painful yet necessary as it was ordered by the high court to maintain peace, law and order till the judgment come out."

People of the Hindu community arranged a memorial meeting for the dead volunteers on April 4, 1991 at the Boat Club, New Delhi, which attracted a large audience. They explained in detail about the happening. They also launched a nationwide awareness program displaying the Asthi Kalash (funeral urns) of those who died in the firing incident. In the following years, these organizations and their prominent leaders received both political and moral endorsement. And, on 6 December 1992, a large group volunteers completely demolished Babri Masjid.

1992 Bombay Riots
The Bombay riots usually refers to the riots in Mumbai, during two months, December 1992 and January 1993. It took the life of approximately 900 people in Mumbai. The riots were mainly due to the escalations of hostilities after large scale protests by Muslims in reaction to the 1992 Babri Masjid Demolition by Hindu volunteers in Ayodhya.

The violence was widely reported as having been orchestrated by the Shiv Sena, a Hindu-nationalist political party in Maharashtra. Learning from the past incidents of India, Shiv Sena, willing to fix its root among Marathi Hindus, staged this violence in the heart of Mumbai, then Bombay. This violence arrested the attention of many humanitarian people of the world.

A lot of talk happened on this, a lot of survey was done, many movies were made, but the fact remaining unchanged could not damage the stand of the instigator – the political party. A high-ranking member of the special branch later stated that the police were fully aware of the Shiv Sena's capabilities to commit acts of violence, and that they had incited hate against the minority communities.

Historian Barbara Metcalf has stated that the riots were anti-Muslim pogrom. The riots were followed by the retaliatory 12 March 1993 Bombay Bombings. The Bombay riots can be considered a result of larger communal tensions throughout India. The British colonial policy of Divide and Rule allegedly included administrative and political activities such as communalized census taking, and the Morley Minto reforms, that relied on communal segregation, and in particular Hindu-Muslim divisions.

Post-Independence, the after-effects of the Partition of India along communal lines, the resurgence of 'Hindu Muslim Economic competition', the growth of right-wing communalist movements such as the RSS, and political strategies of 'appeasement' towards communal political influences by secular political authorities, reinforced communalist ideologies in the country. The Babri Mosque demolition on 6

December 1992, an act of communal violence by Hindu extremist, is considered to be the immediate cause of the riots. As determined by the government's Srikrishna commission; the riots started as a result of communal tension prevailing in the city after the Babri Mosque demolition on 6 December 1992. The Commission identified two phases to the riots. The first was mainly a Muslim instigation as a result of the Babri Masjid demolition in the week immediately succeeding 7 December 1992 led by political leaders representing Hindutva in the city of Ayodhya.

The second phase was a Hindu backlash occurring as a result of the killings of Hindu Mathadi Kamgar (workers) by Muslim fanatics in Dongri, an area of South Bombay, stabbing of Hindus in Muslim majority areas and burning of six Hindus, including a disabled girl in Radhabai Chawl. This phase occurred in January 1993, with most incidents reported between 6 and 20 January.

Looking into the fact, we find that the Report asserted that the communal passions of the Hindus were aroused to fever pitch by the inciting writings in print media, particularly Saamna and Navaakal which gave exaggerated accounts of the Mathadi murders and the Radhabai Chawl incident. From 8 January 1993, many riots occurred between Hindus led by the Shiv Sena and Muslims potentially funded by the Bombay underworld at that time.

An estimated 575 Muslims and 275 Hindus were killed at the end of the riot. The communal violence and rioting triggered off by the burning at Dongri and Radhabhai Chawl, and the following retaliatory violence by Shiv Sena was hijacked by local criminal elements whose potential opportunity was to make quick gains. By the time the right wing Hindu organization, Shiv Sena realized that enough had been done by way of "retaliation", the violence and rioting was beyond the control of its leaders who had to issue an appeal to put an end to it. News of the demolition of Babri Masjid spread by 14:30 hours on 6 December 1992. Muslims angered by this act felt that Islam was in imminent danger since proponents of the Hindu nation had been allowed to destroy, under the very nose of the police forces, the Babri Masjid, despite assurances and undertakings by the Uttar Pradesh state Government and the Government of India that no harm would be permitted to be caused to the Babri Masjid.

The extensive media coverage, particularly on television, of footage of file pictures of Hindus dancing on the dome of the Masjid, as well as the latest video shots showing actual demolition of the Babri Masjid, caused a sense of deep resentment. The demolition of the Babri Masjid provided enough fuel to excite, ignite and exploit the sentimentalities of the Indian Muslims. Muslims were proselytized by these exploitative elements that the Establishment and the Government had an active hand in the destruction, since it did not do anything to prevent the same. Rumors abounded that alleged members of certain Hindutva parties were seen to be celebrating the demolition of Babri structure. Muslims protested violently on the streets. A large number of Muslims congregated near Minara Masjid in Pydhonie jurisdiction in South Mumbai at about 23:20 hours on 6 December 1992 and came out protesting frenziedly. The first targets of the rioting mob became the municipal vans and the constabulary, both visible signs of the government.

Activists of Bharatiya Janata Party and Shiv Sena jumped into the fray, and escalated communal sentiments, as seen from their act of stopping the vehicles on roads in the jurisdiction of V.P. Road Police Station. In Nirmal Nagar jurisdiction, a Ganesh idol in the Ganesh Mandir on Anant Kanekar Marg was found moved out from its place of installation though the lock on the grill surrounding the sanctum was found intact. This was noticed at about 23:45 hours.

At the time the incident happened, there were no immediate clues as to the identity of the miscreants. It was widely rumored that Muslim fanatics were behind it. Following the rumor, in the jurisdiction of Deonar, there was a sharp counter–reaction by Muslims who stoned the house of a local Bharatiya Janata Party leader.

Two constables in Deonar jurisdiction were killed with choppers and swords by the rampaging Muslims, while one lay on the ground bleeding to death, the body of another was dragged and thrown into the garbage heap from where it was recovered seven days later. One constable was done to death in Byculla jurisdiction. Several police officers and policemen who bravely attempted to stem the tide sustained injuries in mob action.

Jogeshwari area, which has been the hotbed of frequent communal riots, saw serious riots at the junction of Pascal Colony and Shankar Wadi. A police officer on duty received a bullet injury in his head and died subsequently, though it cannot be said with certitude that it was a case of private firing. The police recovered large number of iron rods, sickles, choppers, knives and soda water bottles from different jurisdictions indicating that there was intention and preparations to carry on the communal riots.

A violent Muslim mob ransacked a Police station at Maulana Shaukat Ali Road and physically assaulted one Police constable, Pandit Malhari Ahire. Ahire was attacked with swords and choppers and suffered grievous injuries. At about the same time a huge Muslim mob of about 4,000–5,000 collected on Maulana Shaukat Ali Road and in the lanes and by–lanes of the area. The mob went on damaging and destroying the vehicles and public property and indulged in throwing stones.

Ahire's life was saved by prompt action by Senior Police Inspector Pawar along with other officers who carried on firing to restore peace. On 8 December 1992 communal rioting and communal violence spread to 33 jurisdictions, the number of clashes of rioting mobs with police as well as rioting mobs increased alarmingly. Attacks on places of worship also continued. Shiv Sena systematically attacked Muslim men, women and children during that time.

The police had to resort to firing in 43 cases resulting in the death of 11 Hindus, 31 Muslims and three others. There were several cases of mob violence, stabbing and arson. One temple in Dharavi, one in Deonar, one in Park Site and one in Saki Naka were attacked. Simultaneously, two mosques in Dharavi, one madrasa in Mahim and Bhoiwada each and one dargah in Dadar was also attacked.

Though the police found their resources stretched, they were unwilling to take the help of army for carrying out operational duties. Army columns were used only to carry out flag marches which had little impact on the, by now hardened and emboldened, rioters. The imposition of curfew from the night of 7 December 1992 also did not appear to deter the clashing mobs in view of its effete enforcement. Police intervention came about by resort to fire on 72 occasions, killing 15 Hindus and 72 Muslims and injuring 131 Muslims and one Christian.

By the 10th December, the situation had improved further with the number of police stations affected coming down to four, though serious communal riots occurred in Dharavi and Mahim,police jurisdictions to control, and the police had to fire on three and two occasions respectively. By the 12th December, the situation showed further enhancement and the number of police stations affected came down to 14, though there also the occurrences were stray. There were three instances of police firing, one each in

Ghatkopar, Bhandup and Dindoshi. Mob violence took the toll of one life. There were six cases of stabbing. There were eight stray cases of arson. Four dead bodies, all of Muslims, having multiple stab wounds on vital organs and in highly decomposed condition, were recovered from a gutter in Golibar area. However, beneath the surface there was simmering discontent and seething anger amongst the Muslims that unduly excessive police firing had resulted in large number of Muslim casualties. Media had criticized the police for having used unnecessary and excessive fire–power, going so far as to suggest that Muslims were intentionally targeted and selectively killed. This refrain was repeated by political leaders and ministers, past and current.

The explanation of the commissioner of police that the aggressive and violent mobs in the initial stages comprised Muslims and therefore, Muslim casualties were higher. Considering it from all aspects, the Commission was not inclined to give serious credence to the theory that dis–proportionately large number of Muslim deaths in December 1992 was necessarily indicative of an attempt on the part of the police to target and liquidate Muslims because of bias.

On 20 December 1992, two Muslims were locked inside a room in Goregaon, and the room was set on fire as a result of which they suffered severe burns resulting in the death of one. Two bodies, one of a male Hindu and another identified as that of a uniformed Muslim police constable attached to the Nasik Rural Police Headquarters, were recovered from the septic tank of the public latrine in Behrampada on 20 and 21 December 1992 respectively. These bodies bore multiple stab injuries. It would appear that there was a systematic attempt to stab and murder Hindus and the policeman. From 20 January 1993 onwards there was no major communal incident despite a few stray cases being reported. A call was given out by Imam of Jama Masjid that Muslims should boycott the Republic Day and hoist black flags on their establishments and houses. Police maintained continued vigil along with the army and paramilitary forces.

During the subsequent period in January, the situation in the city slowly comes back to normalcy. The total number of deaths was 900. The causes for the deaths are police firing (356), stabbing (347), arson (91), mob action (80), private firing (22) and other causes (4). The violence was widely reported as having been orchestrated by the Shiv Sena, a Hindu-nationalist political party in Maharashtra. A high-ranking member of the special branch later stated that the police were fully aware of the Shiv Sena's capabilities to commit acts of violence, and that they had incited hate against the minority communities. Historian Barbara Metcalf has stated that the riots were anti-Muslim pogrom.

Bal Thackeray, the then-leader of the Shiv Sena, was arrested in July 2000 for his complicity in the riots and for 'inflammatory writings' that may have helped propagate the riots. But the case went loose, and it was later dismissed. Justice Srikrishna, then a relatively junior Judge of the Bombay High Court, accepted the task of investigating the causes of the riots, something that many of his colleagues had turned down. For five years until 1998, he examined victims, witnesses and alleged perpetrators. Detractors came initially from left quarters who were wary of a judge who was a devout and practicing Hindu. The Commission was disbanded by the Shiv Sena led government in January 1996 and on public opposition was later reconstituted on 28 May 1996; though when it was reconstituted, its terms of reference were extended to include the Bombay bomb blasts that followed in March 1993.

The report of the commission stated that the tolerant and secular foundations of the city were holding even if a little shakily. Justice Srikrishna indicted those he alleged as largely responsible for the second phase of the bloodshed and to some extent the first, the Shiv Sena. The report was criticized as "politically motivated". For a while, its contents were a closely guarded secret and no copies were available. The Shiv Sena government rejected its recommendations. Since under the Commissions of Inquiry Act, an Inquiry is not a court of law (even if it conducts proceedings like a court of law) and the report of an inquiry is not binding on Governments, Srikrishna's recommendations cannot be directly enforced.

To date, the recommendations of the Commission have neither been accepted nor acted upon by the Maharashtra Government. Many indicted policemen were promoted by the government and indicted politicians continue to hold high political office even today. Only 3 convictions happened in the 1992-93 Bombay riots cases. On 10 July 2008, a Mumbai court sentenced former Shiv Sena MP Madhukar Sarpotdar and two other party activists to a year's rigorous imprisonment in connection with the riots. However, he was immediately granted bail.

Chapter 12
Anna Hazare Movement Supported by RSS

The Indian anti-corruption movement, commencing in 2011, was a series of demonstrations and protests across India intended to establish strong legislation and enforcement against perceived endemic political corruption. The movement was named among the "Top 10 News Stories of 2011" by Time magazine and other media sources.

The movement gained momentum from 5 April 2011, when anti-corruption activist Anna Hazare began a hunger strike at the Jantar Mantar in New Delhi. It was carried on longer than a week. The chief legislative aim of the movement was to alleviate corruption in the Indian government through introduction of the Jan Lokpal Bill. Another aim, spearheaded by Ramdev, was the repatriation of black money from Swiss and other foreign banks.

Grievances of mass protesters focussed on legal and political issues, including political corruption, kleptocracy, and other forms of corruption. The movement was primarily one of non-violent civil resistance, featuring demonstrations, marches, acts of civil disobedience, hunger strikes, and rallies, as well as the use of social media to organise, communicate, and raise awareness. The protests were nonpartisan and most protesters were hostile to attempts made by political parties to use them to strengthen their own political agendas.

Team Anna is now embroiled in another controversy. The RSS chief, Mohanrao Bhagwat, has said that although the RSS never actively supported the Jan Lokpal movement, it was the RSS that urged Anna Hazare to go on the anti-corruption crusade. The RSS leader also claims that they had spoken to Baba Ramdev as well on starting an anti-corruption movement.

In an interaction with journalists in Kolkata, Bhagwat claimed that Hazare's association with the RSS goes back a long way, and that Hazare used to visit and train RSS cadres in Maharashtra. Bhagwat admitted that RSS activists were present in the Ramlila grounds when the anti-corruption crusade was at its peak.

IBNLive reported that the RSS chief had said, "If asked to, we will participate in the movement, but no request has come from Anna." Congress leader Digvijaya Singh has been alleging that Hazare has a nexus with BJP-RSS in the anti-corruption agitation, and claimed that he had enough evidence to substantiate his allegations.

"The links between Anna and the RSS go back a long way. It was the RSS that highlighted Anna's developmental programmers for villages. We even got Anna to help us in our village development programmers. It was during these interactions that the RSS suggested to him to go in for a movement against corruption. I was supposed to meet Anna in June but both of us got held up elsewhere."

Bhagwat went on to say that the RSS backs Hazare and his movement, and that it will do so in the future as well. The RSS, he said, as an organization, believes in creating better individuals who would lead corruption-free lives. The Congress leader had alleged that the anti-corruption agitation by Hazare and Baba Ramdev were part of an overall plan of RSS-BJP to divert attention from the Sangh's "terror links" and warned spiritual guru Sri Sri Ravishankar that he too could be used by them.

The All India Congress Committee General Secretary said that while Ramdev and Hazare were plan A and B of the Sangh-BJP, Sri Sri Ravishankar is Plan C and asked the spiritual guru to be "wary" of the two organizations. Singh remarked on the microblogging site Twitter "Plan A, B and C are of Sangh and BJP to divert the minds of the people from their involvement in terror activities to corruption. Anna Hazare and his team have so far denied any links with the RSS.

Issues regarding corruption in India have become increasingly prominent in recent years. The country was subject to socialist-inspired economic policies dating from independence in 1947 until the 1980s. Over-regulation, protectionism, and government ownership of industry led to slow economic growth, high unemployment, and widespread poverty. This system of bureaucratic control by government is called the License Raj and lies at the core of endemic corruption.

The Vohra Report of 1993, submitted by the former Indian Union Home Secretary Narinder Nath Vohra, studied the issue of the criminalization of politics. The report contained several observations made by official agencies on the criminal network which was running a parallel government. It also discussed criminal gangs who enjoyed the patronage of politicians and the protection of government functionaries. It revealed that political leaders had become leaders of street gangs and rogue elements in the military. Over the years, criminals had been elected to local bodies, State Assemblies, and the Parliament.

The Right to Information Act (RTI) of 2005 helped civilians work effectively towards tackling corruption. It allows Indian citizens to request information, for a fixed fee of rupees 10 (US$0.22), from a "public authority" (a body of Government or "instrumentality of State"). In turn, this public authority is required to reply to the request within thirty days. Activists have used this to uncover corruption cases against various politicians and bureaucrats — one consequence being that some of those activists have been attacked and even killed by the goons of the politicians. The incidents of such killings mainly happened in metropolitan cities like Delhi and Mumbai.

In the years immediately preceding the 2011 anti-corruption protests there were various notable examples of alleged corruption in the country. These included the Adarsh Housing Society Scam, the 2010 housing loan scam, the Radia tapes controversy, and the 2G spectrum case. In February 2011, the Supreme

Court of India ordered all trial courts in the country to expedite handling of corruption cases and the President of India, Pratibha Patil, stated that measures to ratify the United Nations Convention Against Corruption and other legislative and administrative measures necessary to improve transparency would be taken. A month later, Chief Vigilance Commissioner P.J. Thomas was forced to resign on charges of corruption by the Supreme Court.

A worldwide 50-city Dandi March 2, organized by People for Lok Satta, took place in March 2011 as did the "Drive around Delhi" protest. Dandi March 2 was a march organized by a group of NRIs living in the United States of America inspired by the original march by Gandhi. It is a 240 mile walk in the US against corruption in India from 12 March to 26 March 2011. Starting at Martin Luther King Jr. Memorial Park, San Diego, California March 12, "Dandi March II" goes through Los Angeles and ends March 26 at Gandhi Statue, San Francisco. The dates coincide with the dates Gandhi did his historic march in 1930. Every major city in US, 10 cities in India and 8 other countries are organizing support events on 26 March to extend their support for the full 240 mile walk in US. The agenda was to push the government to enact Jan Lokpal Bill which is drafted to free India from the clutches of corruption by social activists like Kiran Bedi, Anna Hazare, and Arvind Kejriwal.

Anna Hazare wanted a joint committee to be formed, comprising members of the government and of civil society, to draft tougher anti-corruption legislation. Manmohan Singh, then Prime Minister of India, rejected Hazare's demand and so Hazare began a hunger strike on 5 April 2011 at Jantar Mantar in Delhi. He said that the fast would continue until the legislation was enacted. His action attracted considerable support, including some people who joined him in fasting. Prominent representatives of opposition political parties, including the Bharatiya Janata Party and the Communist Party of India (Marxist), indicated their support for Hazare and demanded government action. Hazare would not allow politicians to sit with him and those who tried to join, such as Uma Bharti and Om Prakash Chautala, were turned away.

Protests in sympathy with Hazare spread to various Indian cities, including Bangalore, Mumbai, Chennai, and Ahmedabad. Prominent figures from Bollywood, sports and business indicated their support and there were also gatherings outside India, including in the US, Britain, France and Germany.

The government squabbled with the activists, insisting that the drafting committee would be headed by a government-appointed minister and not a civil society member as the protesters had demanded to avoid allowing the government to make the bill less powerful. On 6 April, Agriculture Minister Sharad Pawar resigned from the group of ministers that had been charged with reviewing the draft bill. Hazare had accused him of being corrupt. On 9 April, the government agreed to establish a joint committee. This came from a compromise that there would be a politician chairman, Pranab Mukherjee, and an activist non-politician co-chairman, Shanti Bhushan. Bhushan was one of the original drafters of the Lokpal Bill along with Hazare, Justice N. Santosh Hegde, advocate Prashant Bhushan and RTI activist Arvind Kejriwal.

The first meeting of the Lokpal Bill drafting committee was held on 16 April. The government agreed to audio-record the committee's meetings and to hold public consultations before a final draft was prepared but refused Hazare's demand that the proceedings be televised live. Ramdev had announced in April that he would launch a people's anti-corruption movement called Bharat Swabhiman Andolan. On 13 May it was announced that India had completed ratification of the UN Convention against Corruption, a process that had begun in 2010. Then, in the early days of June, four senior Union Ministers – Pranab Mukherjee, Kapil Sibal, Pawan Kumar Bansal and Subodh Kant Sahay – met Ramdev to discuss his concerns.

Ramdev supported Hazare's fast and subsequently led a second major protest at the Ramlila Maidan, New Delhi on 4 June 2011. He intended to highlight the need for legislation to repatriate black money deposited abroad. He demanded that such untaxed money should be declared to be the wealth of the nation and, further, that the act of caching money alleged to have been obtained illegally in foreign banks should be declared a crime against the state.

The Ramlila Maidan was booked for 40 days to allow the protest to happen. Preparations included setting up toilet, drinking water and medical facilities, as well as a media centre.[48] Ramdev claimed that more than 100 million people were directly involved with the Bharat Swabhiman Andolan. Almost 3.2 million "netizens" joined the campaign. On 5 June, police raided the Maidan, detaining Ramdev and removing his supporters after firing tear gas shells and lathicharging. 53 people, including 20 police officers, were treated for injuries. Finance Minister Pranab Mukherjee called the police action "unfortunate" but added that the government had to do that as Ramdev had no permission to hold the protest.[53] Ministers said that permission had been granted for a yoga camp with 5,000 attendees but not for a political protest that had gathered 65,000 people.

It was alleged that the action was not a spontaneous decision but had been planned for several days. The police said Ramdev had been informed shortly beforehand that permission to continue his agitation had been cancelled. By that time, over 5000 police officers had been prepared for action. There was an allegation that CCTV footage of the raid was missing. On 6 June, the National Human Rights Commission of India requested that reports of the events be provided within two weeks by the Union Home Secretary, Delhi Chief Secretary and the Delhi City Commissioner of Police. Hazare responded to the events by holding a one-day hunger strike. Protests were held in many parts of country, including the cities of Chennai, Bangalore, Mumbai, Hyderabad, Jammu, and Lucknow. They also spread to Nepal.

Since this uprising, the Congress started losing its ground and the BJP started emerging as the next option. In the year of 2013, Modi became the final face of BJP. Meanwhile, Arwind Kejriwal made his own party and got prominent as an anti-corruption crusader. The BJP sense the threat from Kejriwal's Aam Aadmi Party. Winning in the legislative election of Delhi, Kejriwal became the Chief Minister of Delhi having minority government. He took office on 28 December 2013 but resigned 49 days later, on 14 February 2014, stating he did so because of his minority government's inability to pass his proposed anti-corruption legislation due to a lack of support from other political parties. His resignation made him lose his faith in public. It also gave a rise to Narendra Modi in the next election for the post of the Prime Minister of India.

Chapter 13
The Watchman (Chawkidar) is a Thief

During the general of 2019, the slogan, 'The watchman is a thief' was used by the Indian National Congress. In several election campaigns, the slogan was used by the Congress and some allies. The slogan was coined by the ex INC president, Rahul Gandhi, against the ruling Bharatiya Janata Party (BJP) affiliated sitting Prime Minister Narendra Modi, after raising allegations of favoritism and price escalation in the Dassault Rafale deal. The slogan was coined with the intention of conveying that the person who was entrusted with safeguarding public money (i.e. the watchman) was in fact a thief; context being that Modi had in past claimed to be a "chowkidar" of the nation.

Narendra Modi has often referred to himself as a "chowkidar" (watchman) inferring that he would not allow any corruption in the country. While campaigning for the 2014 Indian general election, Modi in his speeches had promised that he would serve the country, not as a Prime Minister, but as a watchman. Modi further added that as a watchman he would never allow anyone to put their paws on the public money. Rahul Gandhi had referred to Modi as chowkidar during his campaign for the 2017 Gujarat Legislative Assembly election.

The BJP government has denied any wrongdoing in the Rafale deal and the case is being heard by the Supreme Court of India. Gandhi in one of his rallies compared it with BJP's 2014 Indian general election slogan "Achhe din aane waale hain" by stating slogan "Achhe din aayenge" changed to "Chowkidar chor hai". Later in Nagpur, Gandhi stated that an enquiry will be done after the election post which, "the Chowkidar will go to jail".

On 20 November Gandhi commented that a crime thriller titled "Chowkidar hi chor hai" is being played out in Delhi and in its most recent episode, the Central Bureau of Investigation (CBI) Deputy inspector general of police, Manoj Sinha had made allegations of corruption against senior government officials in his affidavit to the Supreme Court, meanwhile his "partner from Gujarat" was amassing enormous wealth. Sinha had stated that government officials and ministers were interfering in the investigation against CBI special director Rakesh Asthana.

On 18 November 2018, during a BJP election rally in Chhindwara, Madhya Pradesh, responding to the repeated chowkidar chor hai slogan against him, Modi stated that the "Naamdaar" (dynast) and the Congress party were hurling abuses at him. On 24 December 2018, Shiv Sena chief Uddhav Thackeray while addressing a rally in Maharashtra state's Pandharpur town, repeated the slogan "Chowkidar chor hai". He elaborated the slogan with a story about a farmer whose Neem plants were attacked by the pests. This was unusual because Neem tree extracts are traditionally used in India for repelling the pests. Thackeray then stated that "this is what is happening everywhere and even those, tasked with protection, are stealing these days."

On 25 March, the slogan Chowkidar chor hai was raised by the audience during the fourth cricket match of IPL 2019 at Jaipur. Later, Modi responded to the jibe by launching a campaign with the slogan "Main Bhi Chowkidar" means 'I too am a watchman' for his supporters, implying that everyone is a fighter against corruption and social evils. Modi even changed the name of his official Twitter handle titled 'Narendra Modi' to 'Chowkidar Narendra Modi'.

In a coordinated campaign, ministers, party president Amit Shah and other BJP leaders such as Piyush Goyal changed their Twitter profile names by adding a prefix "Chowkidar". Many supporters of BJP also changed their names accordingly. Modi addressed a large group of watchmen on audio link as part of the campaign. Congress party criticized BJP's election slogan with Gandhi stating that the truth cannot change since Chowkidar Chor Hai. The chief spokesperson of Congress, Randeep Surjewala responded to Modi's slogan and accused Modi of being the "only chowkidar who is a thief". Congress social media team responded with the slogan "Main Bhi Berozgar" (I too am jobless) to highlight the problem of unemployment under the Modi government and to counter Main Bhi Chowkidar campaign.

Aam Aadmi Party chief Arvind stated that Modi wants the entire country to become 'chowkidar', people who want their children to become watchmen should vote for Modi while those looking for good education for the children to become doctor, engineer or lawyer should vote for the Aam Aadmi Party. BJP leader Meenakshi Lekhi filed a case in the Supreme Court of India seeking a contempt action against Gandhi for misattributing his remarks to the top court. On 22 April 2019, Gandhi filed his response to the Supreme Court's notice on his comments on the sub-judice case of the Rafale fighter jet deal, saying he had attributed the chowkidar chor hai remarks to the Supreme Court "in the heat of the campaign".

In his reply, Rahul Gandhi said he got carried away while campaigning and "unfortunately", the media "mingled" his words. He expressed regret for dragging the top court's name into the comments he made a week ago and also admitted that the Supreme Court had never used the phrase chowkidar chor hai, which he reiterates at every campaign rally accusing Modi of stealing from the poor and handing doles to the rich. Politics is, above all, a battle of narratives, and Narendra Modi has always been a narrative-builder. The notion of the "Gujarat Model", for example, was created out of almost nothing and swept him into power in 2014. During the election of that year, Manmohan Singh had said, "I think it will be disastrous for the country to have Narendra Modi as the PM". Heckled by a section of the media, he declared that history would treat him and his Congress government more kindly. On both counts, his words turned out to be prophetic.

How indeed was he so sure that Modi would be a disaster? Did he know the real nature of Modi and his interest of work for the nation? We may never get to know the answer because Manmohan Singh, contrary to what many had hoped, had no plans to write a tell-all memoir. "I believe I should not write a book in public interest," he had explained without elaborating. But he did add as an afterthought, "Somebody someday will write a book on Narendra Modi and his disastrous government." the conspiracy against my government."

Four and a half years later, his words appear prophetic as the Modi government lurches from one self-made crisis to another. Narendra Modi himself appears diminished, a caricature of his old self. Cracking a joke directed at him would have been unthinkable earlier. But cartoons, memes and jokes on him now abound and stand-up comics are increasingly mimicking him despite the backlash and trolling by the faithful. The bully in Modi is still there, and he has not lost any of his bluster, but the effect is just not the same. The craze is not as it was before.

Modi also sounds like a cantankerous, old man. Responding to the debate on the no-confidence motion in the Lok Sabha, he famously referred to Rahul Gandhi walking across the aisle and giving him a bearhug as the Congress president's unseemly haste to occupy his seat. It sounded like a Freudian slip. Unable to explain the dramatic rise in bank NPAs and bank frauds, he now darkly hints that the economy was in a far worse state than he suspected when he took over.

He also sounds increasingly more bitter and acrimonious. At times, on certain issues, he keeps dubious silence as if he is neither in the support nor in the objection. Unable to tell the country that he has made mistakes or his government has mismanaged the economy, he has taken to finding scapegoats everywhere. No Prime Minister before Modi has invested so much in projecting himself. Every time he goes out, a 40-member crew from state broadcaster DoorDarshan is deployed to beam the event live. As if on cue, all private TV channels pick it up, often without acknowledging the source of the feed or the footage. He has relied on hope and hype to build a larger-than-life image. An expensive publicity machine grinds 24x7 to promote him through events, billboards, TV time, Radio talks, print advertisements, social media, WhatsApp and his seemingly endless travel.

The economy is a shambles; the prices of essential commodities and fuel have gone through the roof, the Rupee is at an all-time low, manufacturing and exports have declined, corruption in government offices remain the same, jobs are harder to get, trains no longer run on time and criticism of the PM even on Facebook or Twitter is enough to land one in jail.

....

Cromosys Publication's

The Parliament Horror

Niranjan Jha Showman

The End

NIRANJAN JHA SHOWMAN

Founder - Niranjan Jha Showman

Education and Technology Research Center

Patankar Park, Nallasopara (W), Mumbai. +91-9561450045

Education, Technology, Publication, Healthcare, Newsmedia, Realtor, Filmmaking

www.facebook.com/cromosys

Cromosys Publication
Teach
Yourself
German
NIRANJAN JHA SHOWMAN

Cromosys Publication
Teach Yourself French
NIRANJAN JHA SHOWMAN

Cromosys Publication
Teach
Yourself
Spanish
NIRANJAN JHA SHOWMAN

Cromosys Publication

English
Voice
Accent and
Pronunciation

NIRANJAN JHA SHOWMAN

Teach
Yourself
Autodesk
MAYA
Cromosys Publication
NIRANJAN JHA SHOWMAN

Cromosys Publication
Teach
Yourself
Autodesk
3ds Max
NIRANJAN JHA SHOWMAN

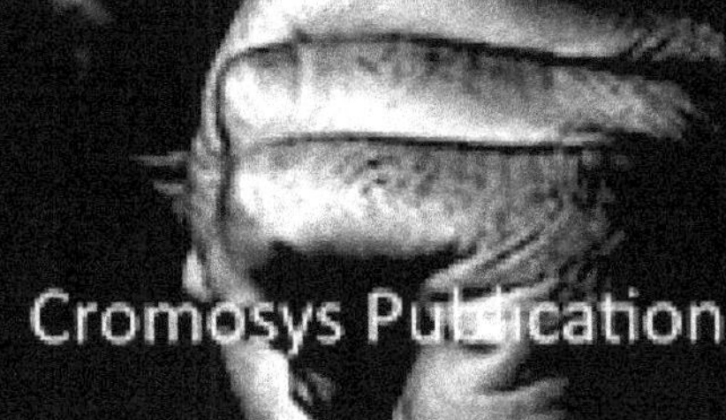

Cromosys Publication

CRIMINAL FACTORY

NIRANJAN JHA SHOWMAN

Cromosys Publication
FOCAL DISASTER
NIRANJAN JHA SHOWMAN

Cromosys Publication
Your talents will not help you succeed without your skill of using them.
NIRANJAN JHA SHOWMAN
BE MILLIONAIRE LIKE ME